MW01518943

poems and short stories

by

Nash Consing

contents

The next page that you will read is the beginning of a story; my story. Yours, too. It will soon be ours. Although this story may seem grand—although it may leave an imprint on you as permanent as ink on this page—it is a story that will not last forever. It will end. We are small. 'Forever' may mean forever to you and me, but to others it is nothing but a moment suspended in time before reality begins moving again. This is what this story is. This is what we were, are, and will be. This book is a forever that will last for infinity and not at all—at the same exact time. This is the story of how we fell in love; how we fell out of it; and how we forgot about its entire existence. This is the story of the next us, the one after that—and so on. If 'us' was formerly you and I, we are still 'us' if it is just me; if it is just you. This story was a forever to two people—at least for a moment in eternity. Although this is a forever that ends, it will live forever. This is how. It is just a speck of ink among a sentence among a paragraph among a chapter among an entire novel. This is what we are. It may be uncomfortable to some, but it is definitely necessary to the completion of our entire lifetimes. So—this is us. A forever suspended in time; a pause; a silence,

   —to the reader, writer, and doer,
        —from the past, present, and future

AND THEN THERE WAS US,

first off

A thousand thoughts run through my mind
the minute I hear your name
and although it's just the beginning
I know my heart
will never be the same

freeze:

here comes the story
that you will one day
soon forget;
the dates
the faces
the sequences of events

yet
you will arrive
at this particular memory
day in and day
out
and you will think of
us,
whoever that may be
by tomorrow.

seventeenth

We found each other in a lunch line. I was antisocial and she was exuberant. People looked at me and her and they saw a shy-and-awkward-and-tanned-skin-from-the-summer boy and a short-but-loud-and-energetic-and-red-from-the-sun girl and they didn't bother to look twice. The only ones who did were the two of us.

She read books and looked at flowers; I liked rap and produced art in heartbreak. A normal person in speculation would think that flowers don't go well with heartbreak, but they would have never guessed that between us two they did.

My words. Were. Choppy. I could — say things in — sequences. But hers, they flowed, in motion, andthey waltzed, andthey waltzed, andthey waltzed, allovermy heart. If our voices were puzzle pieces, of course the features of our personalities and styles of speech wouldn't be able to fit together. But somehow the bend in my cardboard had melted its way into hers; it didn't matter how much contrast there was between us. We discovered almost instantaneously that our pieces had fit together perfectly.

The world watched as these two unlikely souls tied themselves in each other's loops around one another without much hesitation at all. We formed into a sculpture that looked like thrift-shop art — yet we received the self-appraisal of professionalism. We were an avant-garde success story in the art of emotion.

From this moment onward, the greatest physical feat could have sought its way to divide us. A thousand miles could grow between us in this lunch line that we were standing in and she would still be looking at me. She would still see the fire in my eyes and the blood flowing through their veins. She had picked my soul and heightened it with a single glance. Anything else that

3,

didn't have to do with her suddenly became duller to me. Although it was the very beginning, we knew that we were going to be together. We smiled in a world that she and I had quieted. This was going to be us. The world was going to be ours.

gasping for air
i have ended up in tranquility
made of quicksand
much so that my heart has slowed to the dynamic of
conversations
that have reached my current ears; pianissimo
it could have been air
but i was not falling
rather, sinking
through a voice
that i could only hear
until i was halfway
underground
and unknowingly
i have caught myself
halfway down; falling

i've been connecting
the dots of the earth's pores
but if i am going to be honest
the lines draw themselves for me;
i smile with sunglasses on
although i have not seen the sky in months
or maybe i am the one who has been
emitting rays through the permafrost
that has suffocated me
for so long
and for the first time
i have found green
in the darkness
of your hands
if only by chance

for before, us

It is silent between us. At least through the dialogue between our quiet throats, it is. Everything around us speaks louder than I can imagine. The engine of my aging car, mumbling unrecognizable phrases, seems to have established an elephant that has grown almost exponentially from the moment you opened the car door up until this final drive back to your house.

The air outside has been constantly throwing itself on us throughout the whole afternoon as if it were watching us, captivated by this episode of me with you like it were the premiere of a television series that would soon win awards for its unrelenting drama and romance; however, I cannot contemplate about the projection of this season debut. I can't even think of what direction I'm heading in when we reach the four way intersection. I can't think of the name of the song that plays twice a day on my car radio CD. It is track five when my eyes point over to the dash, but when I look down at track five's display on my 2003ed car radio, I don't look at the radio at all. I've just made an attempt to look at you, and that is as good as my eyes can do without turning my head towards your direction.

But the desire to just observe you screams too loud for the stiffened muscles in my neck to stay still.

So I look at you. And you look at me, and you laugh, and so do I, because we both don't know what exactly to say to one another about what exactly we just experienced together.

There are things that I should say. And there are things you probably want to as well, although I can't really tell what's on your mind. 'Maybe Next Time' becomes my friend, and I'm hoping, in the smallest of hopes, that you've become friends with 'Maybe Next Time' too.

Because the elephant keeps growing inside of this car and the weight of its body continues to build on top of my heart as you tell me, "Thanks for the time, I had fun," and then wait for a couple seconds before opening the car door just to see if I have anything in particular that I want to say. But I don't say a word—I'm already too stunned by your existence. If there is anything you or I need to say to each other, it won't happen tonight. It might not ever happen. But maybe I'll let the silence speak for itself. And I'll hope tonight was a shy, subliminal *almost* for us.

A pause; before our hearts begin intertwining.

ninety degrees

i will hold your sides
and you will stare into my eyes
as if the hands
in the possession of your body
have ripped the cells of your skin
apart
just to feel closer
to the pulsation
of the heart
that has always
screamed
yours

green wheels

You are sitting in the third row of a car. It is nighttime; you're on your way home. Your three friends in the middle seats are knocked out. The couple of the group are in their own conversation — in their own world — as they have been and always will. You don't mind it. They don't annoy you. Although they only see each other through their romantic filter most of the time, they still communicate to the rest of the world with open arms.

The girl next to you was never really a part of your group of friends until recently — but then again, neither were you. To the group, the two of you were mutual friends from opposite spectrums of the group; the both of you were friends with all the individuals of the group, but never friends with each other.

So far, it has been casual. Almost platonic — although you hate that word. It reminds you of wet cement. You hate the word especially now because you don't want things to solidify in the 'just friends' way with her. Even though you just met, you're still trying to get to know her. You admit to yourself that she is beautiful — however, you don't tell her this because you think she'll be weirded out. But these are your honest thoughts regardless.

She's been smiling at you the whole night, laughed at your jokes, and became comfortable with your existence. Her conversation even turned real; vulnerable — at least for a moment. She would sometimes look at you in the darkness in a way you used to know with different people who no longer do that to you.

You know what you're thinking even though you know that, for now, it's out of consideration. There are too many variables to start a fire with a handful of twigs. This isn't love at first sight, or even love at first conversation like how it was with other people who have graced your heart. You know that, if anything, this will start gradually.

She's fallen asleep by now; it's only you and the couple who are awake at this point. The presence of her body radiates to the pores of your aching body. She shifts; her knee brushes against yours.

You sigh, look out the window, and wonder if this is the spark that has already ignited you towards her direction knowing that your heart has already been burning for her existence.

outside, in

i only know her
in whispers (my thoughts
yell at her eyes when
ours meet),

and although she may
seem shy (i could exhaust
the dictionary defining her
awkward glances away from
mine),

i have a feeling
that slowly, we will
become friends (my world has
accelerated into a universe
where she exists).

stick back

We were sitting in a crowded room in the middle of June watching a romance film that was probably relevant to our minds but not to our hearts. The only thing relevant was my heart forming inside yours, and maybe you felt the same as your fingers inched closer towards mine. My eyes watched the film, but my mind felt the presence of your soul elevating slowly next to mine.

We would breathe in unison; every inhale drew anticipation, every exhale created an attraction between my skin and yours, and eventually my fingers found your grooves that formed perfectly into mine. I saw you with eyes that fluttered to the pulse of my beating heart, and all of a sudden we weren't two people holding hands on a humid night anymore; we were one connected soul existing on an infinite plane.

This moment wasn't really about how I could feel your diaphragm radiating like the frequencies of our ocean or the way you left a tighter grip when the film became exceedingly graphic. It was about the fact that when you brushed your fingers delicately against my own, sparks ignited out of my heart, a fire was lit under my soul, and the entropy of my thoughts increased inside my mind.

During that summer, time didn't slow down for anyone. But on that night, for us and only us, time was the only thing we had. We were given a brief window of communication that required no vocals chords to be strung. In our temporary world, you and I were one; our hearts were whole; and our souls were enlaced like a scene out of a romance film — a film that lasted an hour and thirty minutes to our eyes, yet it was a movie that would last infinity to our hearts.

when the music slows

when the music slows,
and the energy of the night
submerges down into the hearts
that may or may not have been
emotionally prepared for this moment—
eyes will begin to wander frantically around the venue
in search for their others of significance.

i have always been the one
to interlock my eyes
onto a heart that encompasses
my beating emotions
as the afternoon's pace winds down
for just three minutes;
but i have always passed
on the opportunity
in my greatest fear
of rejection

but tonight
the moon does not paint its reflection
on the lake
in the theme of unrequited love

for when the music slows tonight
my heart will interlock
its scars and bruises and struggles
into the fears and traumas and aches
of her

and i will feel pure
in her arms.

cecilia

We fell in love before we were eighteen. When I told the world, it paused for a second, looked up at us with half of a smile, and said, "Congratulations, I hope you last."

Confused by this reaction, I told the world how we had first met on a random Wednesday on a school campus that was as small as my heart at the time. I tried to define the emotion I felt when I first looked into her eyes. Her pupils were always naturally more dilated than the biological norm and her irises were always naturally more vivid than one could emotionally perceive.

But when I couldn't find the word for the feeling that had planted itself into my vocabulary, the world looked at me with eyes that looked more bored than misunderstood and it said, "What a story. I wish I could have had a high school romance like that."

We fell in love before we were eighteen; I asked the world if it saw the way lightning struck the expression on my face once I saw you. Or if it could feel the temperature of my boiling blood when my fingers started trembling as I touched the bare emotion that had encrypted itself into the pores of your skin. I wondered if it heard the silence that would seemingly last forever in the moments when our lungs stopped running for a split second—just to savor the existence of our lips being pressed together.

The world said, "Yes, that is what always happens to everyone when they are young," with an uncomfortable pause that never had a resolution.

And it came to this moment when I realized that the world didn't care about you or me or us. Because we were in love before we were eighteen; a love that the world knew existed—but never bothered to care about.

The world saw as a young couple that rode on the waves on infatuation—only to eventually crash on the shores of broken maturity.

But the world didn't see the chainmail that you had dressed on my heart. It didn't see the tattoos of your existence that had dissolved into the opening of my soul. It never noticed the grasp of my life that you had taken and meshed inside of yours. And yes—we fell in love before eighteen. But it was a love that wasn't covered in infatuation or materialism. It was a love that allowed me to live as a teenager and an elder at the same time. It had no timestamp. We felt forever already.

fall

the flowers will die
with you by my side
and i can assure you
i'd be the only one lonely

because there are
pinks in our lips
and stems that still stay
but you're the only flower
that can hold me

an average night

It started out as an average night — but it was one out of only a couple in my life that I would be fortunate enough to spend with you.

I was infatuated with every dimension about you; from the first reaction you gave me when we first met, to the conversations we had long after we both figured out that we were just as awkward as each other, to the way I tended to throw out emotional secrets randomly in hopes that you wouldn't view me in any other way — which you didn't, to the way the touch of your fingers against my skin made the nerves in my body more electric than the current of lightning.

In this particular moment in the night, on this spot on the earth, under the stars that rotated around the universe in an infinite measure of space, my infatuation for you continued. I can't remember what we were talking about exactly; maybe I mentioned something about how I missed petting my dogs, or maybe you were discussing the inevitabilities of life, but eventually we ran out of things to say.

In moments like these — especially in moments like these — when two infatuated souls run out of things to say, they let their hearts take control of their bodies and begin to speak through their actions. My heart had a lot to say to yours.

All of a sudden, you and I were engaged in this emotional conversation; an exchange of dialogue without saying a single word. Our bodies were as close as could be, our fingers were as tightly enlaced as the bond we had quickly built, and our lips met in a motion that translated the words any heart in love would long to emote.

As the rest of the world saw this, we were two people out of millions of people that kissed on a seemingly average night. But to us, we were one mind that shared the same heart on a night that I would remember for the rest of my life.

A night when I knew I was infatuated.

A night when I was sure I was in love.

home

we've come from
different cities
but
there's a town
in you and me
and it has
already scraped
the skies of my heart

never forget this, part one

If you ever forget (which—my God, if you ever forget), there are a couple of things that you should know about this temporary moment in your life.

There are these set of eyes that noticed you first. As the days go by, you begin to appreciate the fact that these eyes found you. But unlike most of the eyes you preciously became infatuated with, you do not notice this particular set at first glance. It's only until you see the beauty in this pair of plain blues that you realize that these galaxy-patterned spheres have turned in your direction the same way; every single time; since the beginning of familiarity between your eyes and these eyes.

There is this voice that began as a vocal wave built upon eager nervousness, and you don't understand why at first. But it doesn't take long to grow familiar with the different emotions that travel through the air and arrives in your ears. You know everything from the softness when the voice feels comfortable; to the glow of the excited voice; to the hesitation of the embarrassed one. Every tone is something special to you. You begin to lean in every time the drums in your ears begin to roll once they move in on cue with this voice.

But then, for the first time, you notice a new emotion for the first time from the same voice—an emotion that sounds like it's been held back ever since the day your own voice conversed with this one. It arrives in a whisper that is softer than any dynamic your eardrum has ever handled. And for no reason and for all reasons, you lean in the farthest than any other tone, knowing that you will soon learn that this is your favorite version of this voice.

There are these lips that, at the beginning, only serve as a medium for delivering verbal communication. But lips can only do so much verbally, so these lips begin to trade emotions with yours. To say that you grow accustomed to these lips are unsettling because really you never do. You do, however, begin to long for their touch at every moment you become close to them, even in the slightest of distances. You become addicted to the coding that lies in the grooves of this pair of red flesh. You become mightily attracted to the emotion that devours you when you and these lips conduct a melody that only your soul and the carrier of these lips will know; not because you're infatuated with kissing — or because you're in love with these lips.

Because there's this girl. A girl, at this moment, that you hope isn't temporary. A girl that has become poetry. A girl with a pair of eyes, a voice, and a set of lips — but every girl has a pair of eyes, a voice and a set of lips. This girl has a heart. And at this moment, it's yours too. And you should never forget that.

a moment from time

Time doesn't wait for anyone.

The minute we are born into this world, a moving countdown initiates over our heads — an immediate alarm clock into death; a statement of limitation to our lives. At first, when we are children, we do not know this; but as we grow and form into the time spectrum, we soon uncover that there is only limited time in this world for us to experience.

Tonight began awkwardly, like a model taking her first step with her weight solely on a twisted ankle. There was a lot of talking at the beginning; a lot of smiles, a lot of hugs, and a lot of screams of excitement. One of my fatal flaws included the inability to stir a conversation that would last more than a couple exchanges of a hello, a nod, and then a turn away from the extreme discomfort of the inability to stir a conversation that lasts more than a couple exchanges that la —

You were the one who did the talking; I was just the nodder. No matter what, you stayed by my side. You never said this, but you knew from my face that in a room full of strangers I would be extremely anxious. That's how we met, anyway — in a room full of strangers.

When the music started, so did the dancing. Jackets were put on hanger racks, ties were loosened, and heels were kicked off into the corner of the room. Every pop song on the hit radio station from ten years ago was sputtered into the room and all of a sudden they became as catchy and relevant as they were when the songs first came out. I didn't look around the room too much after that. I just looked at you.

There was then a sudden halt in the atmosphere where all the jaggedness and pop of the night had crept their way out of the room; the music became soft. It turned out to be the only slow song of the night.

When the song began, there was no music at all. There were no people. There was no room that we stood in. There was no school dance that we were once in. There was just you and me.

We stared at each other. Your eyes shuttered as you blinked; a different scene played every time you reopened them.

In our relationship, you usually were the one to talk and I was the shy one. But in this moment, we exchanged no words. With our eyes alone, we told each other everything that had built us in the last half year that we had spent together.

Time doesn't wait for anyone.

It will kill us the minute we are born until the second before we die, and then we will be dead. But there are only a select few moments in our lives where the concept of time, death, inevitability- they all mean nothing in these moments.

The moment when we beat time; the moment when time stands still; is the moment where we enjoy the beauty of living.

And tonight you made me feel alive.

july 24th at one a.m.

We are sitting on a bench at 1 am on the last day of camp. We haven't slept all night — and we don't plan on it either, because staying awake just to be with each other is more valuable than throwing a couple more memories away. The bench is wooden but has the comfortability like that of sitting on rocks. We're layered in sweat from the waves of humidity that has covered us the whole summer. There are a hundred more things we could have complained about, but tonight we don't mind. Because as long as your voice can travel into mine in whispers that scream that it's going to be okay; as long as the human scent of yours floats into my memories and reminds me of your closeness that will physically be taken from me in the next eight hours; as long as the softness of your skin electrifies the beat of my heart; as long as you are with me and I am with you; then nothing else is relevant.

But it's two in the morning. And as all things go — from this point forward — I won't be able to be with you. You'll be able to whisper three plain syllables that will be translated into something significant, but you won't be able to catch me off guard staring across fields of imagination to surprise my lips with my heart's favorite greetings. You won't be able to let me trace your history across the stars made of the marks on your skin. Because it's supposed to be the end. Because what happens in the summer stays in the summer — that's how it's always been.

But although it is a crazy idea to keep each other past these few, temporary weeks, it's insanity to let you go. And though we've never had a conversation about this change, we are about to transition to, you look at me and I look at you. There's infinity in your pupils and there are fields of promise in your irises.

You look at me like camp hasn't ended.

24,

You look at me like our lives just started.

hello, this is my friend

there's no more
difference
between our
"i love you"s
and our goodbyes
because baby
i can feel
your kisses
in my sighs

i'll still hold onto you

People will ask why I'll still hold on to you even after time has passed, long after a comfortable duration, and I can try to explain it to them, but they won't understand. They won't understand the minute I start telling them the big reasons, like the fact that you're a soul worth fighting for; or that nobody else in my city connects to me as well as someone like you; or that loving you means a lot more to me than surrendering myself to the borders of time and distance.

They still won't understand even if I explain the little things that I favor the most about you — like the way you always look into my eyes; or the way you form your fingers around mine while listening to the earth; or even the times you've caught me off guard, and in a sporadic but delicate window of time, you'd lean in and kiss me right as I'd turn back to you.

Nobody will understand about how quickly I fell for you — so quickly in fact, that I actually became scared of falling in love so fast, with as many doubts as there were certainties swirling around my soul about you. I had doubts that included statements that said that things are only temporary, but I had a certainties from day one that you were someone that would last permanently in my state of mind and the fixture of my heart.

Nobody will understand the simple passion I felt as the skin of your arm rested next to mine when we watched summertime films together. Nobody will understand a thing I will tell them; but in retrospect, nobody has ever understood me completely — including the parents that have raised me, the friends that have supported me, and the exes that claim to still know me.

Nobody understood me until you showed up in my life.

And so people will ask why I'll still hold on to you.

And I'll smile and think of you, as you would for me.

return details

To:
Every night
spent without you
with miles and miles
in between us,

For:
Every night
spent sleeping
skin to skin
in the same bed
feeling thankful
that the both of us
were strong.

august 8th

Another sun had set into the clouds today, just as it did every afternoon this summer. Today was the sixty third sunset since you last saw her. I hope you still remember that day.

Everything was soft. The grays on the wall, the pillow that caressed my waking soul, the sheets that hugged on our tranquil bodies; her skin. Even her breath—a warm, pulsating exhale—arrived delicately into your ears, as if you were listening to the ocean come and go in the quiet existence of the winter. Your blinks became louder and louder as you woke. A tragic realization voiced a statement announced that you had to drive back home today.

"Hmm," she muttered, as her subliminal senses realized movement from your body's minute budges.

You sat up slowly, trying not to wake her. She shifted off your chest and curled into a sleepy ball at the edge of the bed, facing you. You looked at her.

There were lines of light from the sun creeping into the blinds of the window across the room that crawled on the left side of her face. Her hair was wavy and frazzled from the sleep last night. It was natural. You always liked that about her hair. It complimented its color—a vast mixture of autumn's leaves and the metal that wrapped around billions of people who swore themselves into a lifetime commitment—there was nothing more natural than that. Her skin was pale; but then it wasn't. Her face was blushed into soft pink, as if she was permanently looking at the clouds, and then one day she decided to look down, only to notice the amount of people looking at her, wondering why her head was in the clouds all this time. Her lips, worn thin from last night's whispering secrets, laugh-worthy moments, and infinite embraces with yours, were at a slight opening, inhaling and exhaling our shared breaths from the last couple of days.

The first thought that landed on your tongue every time that you saw her was that she was simply beautiful. Many times you would tell her that she was. But every time she heard you say these emotions that spilled out of your mouth, she would respond in a way that appreciated your compliments; but at the same time, she was bothered because you said it even though you meant the words that were ricocheting inside of your heart. She would claim that it was okay that things are not beautiful all the time — nobody could ever be beautiful at all times of the day. And at this moment — at the beginning of the morning — she was just plain, not beautiful.

But you had seen this morning version of her before. And you had fallen in love with this version of her as the months had passed.

There was so much beauty in simplicity of things if they meant something significant enough to strike your natural perception. And she pierced straight through yours.

"Goooodmorning," she whispered, a little more awake now. She was a heavier sleeper than you were.

"Good morning, love," you whispered back into her ears. You ran your fingers through her hair.

You cherished the rarity of the moment. You could only experience waking mornings with the one you loved a few times a month, and the softness of the morning could only last so long before both of you were awake and aware of the day ahead. These were the moments that were going to last you through the time that you had to endure without her, cities away, when the miles between you two would grow longer by the desperation and the loneliness of your own thoughts. Her eyes opened. They were a pale blue, and just like her morning breath. The blue in her eyes were faded, as if a coating of snow had fallen into its wavy surface. You saw these eyes for the first time in the summer a year ago, and maybe that's why you did not seem taken by them at first. But days later, when you kissed each other before both of you were really ready, you drowned into a pale blue sea and you didn't sink to the bottom — so you swam there yourself.

"We gotta get ready to go," you urged, as you opened up the bedsheets from their embrace over us. She fought back, and returned the covers over us. You laughed, aware of her grumpiness in the mornings. You complied. The both of you still had time to get ready.

You waited for about ten minutes until she was as awake as you were; a groggy mess, but conscious nonetheless. You sat and stared at the ceiling dotted in white specks like you did last night at the stars. Something crossed your mind; it was something you had been putting off for the entirety of your visit to her because you wanted to absorb the moments you had with a girl that — together — never had enough time to spend.

hardened

lay me down in permanence
with the infrastructure
of our earth
and i will wait
for the mortar to dry
because you are all the worth

before, during, or after

I'll tell you "I love you" early into our relationship because the chances are when I first meet you I'll already be in love with you—consciously or not. Maybe it won't be the first conversation we have; that usually starts out as a "hello my name is..." and then we'll proceed why we want to exist in each other's lives. But there's a difference between talking about our lives and sharing them—and the minute I'll experience yours my heart will instantaneously leap in your direction.

I'll tell you "I love you" early into our relationship because chances are when our heart rates aren't as fast when we see each other like they used to be; when our comfortable silences turn into standard silences; when our statements turn into arguments and all we can ever think of is what is wrong; I'll remember that I actually do love you—that my heart still beats for you; that silence doesn't mean doubt and arguments are only temporary.

I'll tell you "I love you" early into our relationship because when I am no longer yours and you are no longer mine we will argue and fight for an excruciating duration until our blood will flow faster than the devil's river and we will forget every single moment we have ever built. But I will know that at one point in my life, I truthfully loved someone who has unfortunately become unknown to me.

I will tell you "I love you" early on into our relationship most importantly because I will see myself loving you not only before, during, or after our existence; I will see myself loving you infinitely.

tonight I miss you

there is an indistinguishable line
between
heart-achen and heart-broken
tonight.

and although my heart
is meticulously intertwined
between the chambers of your own —
it shakes
as if i were once again alone

but tonight
i just miss you
in my rawest form.

the after effects of the temporary goodbye:

One of the first effects will be the realization of the decrease in the use of your auditory and verbal senses. You will quickly discover that you will physically hear zero "I love you"s from the voice of the one that you intend on hearing directly into your ears. The only ones that you will hear will be through the tolls of technology where the clarity of your partner will be significantly worse than your own and through the realm of imagination and memory—which may play a big part during all the highs and lows of the Temporary Goodbye.

There will be extreme periods of loneliness that will enter your mind. They will come in short, jagged waves at first; they will take stabs at your happiness that you and your significant other have built in the short period of time that you have been together. Gradually, the waves will grow taller, larger, and longer; they may knock you to the inability of normal thought. Often in your sleep, you will reach out your arms in hopes that you will come into contact with smooth skin on a warm body; however, you will find nothing but the cold skeleton of the bed frame.

The most sustaining effect of the Temporary Goodbye will be the growing desperation to see your significant other. At first, this feeling will grow to what seems exponentially worse than anything you have experienced in the past. The pressure in your heart will increase so rapidly that the intensity of heartache will turn from a pebble to a mountain onto your chest. Your mind, usually traveling from point A to point B, will be sprinting in circles trying to find the solution to the emptiness that screams inside of your heart. As the days pass by, the view of the present time will drown. Your memories of the past and your visions of the future will grow intrusively like how cancers spread throughout a body's system. This will be dangerous from the beginning of the Temporary Goodbye to the week before the First Hello. After that pivotal turning, point the air will clear from your lungs and the pressure of your heart will minimize until the holes in your heart a refilled with the Permanent Hello.

But until then, there will be inevitable suffer in the time after the Temporary Goodbye.

with you tomorrow

i may not be with you tonight
but that leaves us no time for sorrow
because even with daily miles
in between us
i will always be with you tomorrow

seeing the storm

"There's a storm coming," she said.

We looked up at the cloud. It was as if a mountain from the sky was on the verge of colliding with the earth. The bottom of the cloud had a golden brown tint. It held the last reflection of the sunlight.

I turned my eyes towards her and I saw her eyes traveling along the cloud from bottom up. The top of the cloud looked as if it was still daytime; however, the sun had already submerged within the tree line that had surrounded us.

"Yeah," I answered nervously. I immediately regretted my response. My second thoughts screamed that I sounded impatient.

She gathered her observations from the sky and retired her thoughts down to a simple smile.

She was fascinating. In the past couple of weeks that I had known her, she was everything that I didn't know could exist in the soul of one human being. In a place as busy as the one we had both chosen to live in, there was a contrast in the way she chose to live and think.

The evolution of our city seemed to change at an interval of a couple minutes. Every day there was someone who made a life changing discovery; an artist who had struck a pickaxe into gold; a businessman who conquered the capitalization of his pursuits; or an engineer who had anchored their life-defined masterwork.

It was a beautiful thing to exist in a city that transformed into a different person every morning—yet remained the same despite these changes.

However, there was a problem of living in a city as temporary as ours. Nothing felt permanent. Most of the people I had known while living here were acquaintances just for a matter of months before never speaking to them again. The lips I kissed often said goodbye; sometimes with regret; sometimes with no remorse; but nonetheless, my lips were worth forgetting. They were just average lips.

But I knew when she looked at me, there was something unexplainable about her. She was one to stop and look at flowers growing in the corner of a skyscraper simply because they were beautiful.

She looked at me with eyes of infinity in a city of limited possessions.

Thunder rumbled above our heads, and a raindrop fell between her lips.

We would see each other by the morning.

are you sure, she asked.

When the sun died in our eyes
and the stinkbugs from Japan decided
that it was time to crawl on the brown upstairs walls for
the winter again
they saw us there for the first time.

Hand on hand,
lips on lips,
arms in arms,
we had tended to a fire
that had ignited with the pine needles
and the box matches
of the summer camp
where we met.

She kissed me and it was different
unfiltered;
there was nobody who was on the lookout
for human contact.

Tongue against mine,
her fingers traveled shakily
in rotation around my world.

She kissed me down from my lips to my neck;
soft hugs;
they were calm.

Are you sure,
She asked.

There are many parts of a relationship.
love me romantically,
love me historically,
love me intellectually,
yes,
yes,
yes.
love me physically,
yes.

Are you sure?

Yes.

As my walls disintegrated into her embrace
the battle that I had been fighting against beauty
was exposed to her.
Was I desirable enough?
Was I attractive enough?

Was I enough?
Romantically, historically, intellectually,
yes.

As she took my hands;
as she let me take off her own shield,
she answered my questions
with the same ones.

She loved me in every way
without question.

Now as the stinkbugs from Japan
come and go for the winter,
they know when we are upstairs
for the walls are painted
in buckets of golden
love
in a room
painted brown.

longing for you is all the worth

I'm lying in bed and my ceiling fan is too loud and the air is too thick and the moonlight is too bright; however, on every other night for the past week, the variables have been the exact same as the ones I lay in this afternoon.

Tonight I miss you. I tell you "I miss you" almost every day; But tonight, the "I miss you"s have seeped my mouth shut; traveled down my lungs; invaded my heart; and suppressed every emotion my heart can contain — except for the feeling of loneliness.

Of course I'm taking you for granted. It's a privilege to ache for someone who aches for you as well. But tonight I miss the way your voice turns from a philosophical conversation to a reassuring whisper that has promised me that everything will work itself out.

Tonight I miss the closeness of your presence that draws a halo around your body — the closeness when we shuffle closer into each other's vicinity and I feel something exclusive about the air I'm inhaling as my body exists next to yours.

Tonight I miss the way the world lightens up every single time you enter my vision — whether it is across the room or from a quarter of a mile away, the grass turns greener and the trees grow taller because the positivity of seeing you smile illuminates my soul.

We both signed up for the aches and the hurts and the pains and maybe that's just us growing through this commitment together. Because when I see you again, I'll be able to hear the velvet coating of your voice. I'll be able to feel the electricity of your presence. I'll be able to see shades of your skin outside of my regular spectrum. When I experience these things, I'll cherish the things I have been taking for granted all this time. But tonight, I will miss you to my heart's greatest capacity. And tonight my ears will scream. And my lungs will wheeze. And my heart will ache.

Because longing for you is all the worth.

47

your voice enters the speakers of my brain
and suddenly

my heart
beats faster
in synchronized choreography

my mind
bounces
in a messy rave

and my vocal chords
slow dance
to the sound of your name

and yet
the music
of my infatuation
for you

has just begun.

art. poetry. you.

My eyes have scratched at the pages of a million different souls searching for the right words to mean something worth holding to me. I have gone through every library in the closest 100 miles and have read the eyes of every genre and none have seemed to touch an ounce of my being. Most of the time the words I've found so far turn out to be fiction.

Since the beginning of our lives, that's all we are taught — and rightfully so. We are taught fiction to survive the emotional streets of the world; to always be aware of protecting the truth to our souls.

But the world is essentially ineffective in the situation where it is okay to expose the vulnerability of the nonfiction that is built in the foundation of our souls. When I looked into the eyes of the majority of the literature I ran into, the only thing I could see was fiction. For the majority of the time, I could read off the lines of the stories once and know what was true to my heart or what was false. There were instances when at times I had found a story that had captured my attention — even ones that captured my heart.

When I thought it was worth the risk, I put my own story onto a blank page in hopes that it could be made for two.

But always, always, always — the stories would end up turning their pages and falsify — sometimes slowly; sometimes swiftly; but always tragically.

But one day, I ran into you and I saw your irises. In them, I found a bibliography of truth. And you said hello — just like how all the other stories started — except that I could feel the wave of warmth rolling off the articulation of your tongue.

Immediately you captivated my heart. You made me feel like I was living in a fantasy — in fiction — except that this was happening in reality. There was compassion in your voice and acceptance in your smile. You told me — without words — during the first time we met that there was much more in the world than true and false; that there was beauty and tragedy in art in everything. In everyone. You told me you saw poetry in me.

And maybe that's what I needed. I needed you. I needed poetry. A mix of truth and fiction, but ultimately art. And ever since then, that is what has captivated me. Art. Poetry. You.

a moment in infinity

light breathing, a slow soul in my hands
expands and returns in constant motion,
skin on skin.
it is warm under these sheets.
morning breath comes naturally
in dampened murmurs
to say
good morning.

the groom is still gray
but yellow lines have streaked their way
along the edges of the wall
and instantly jag at its corners.

across the room,
a blurry clock hangs above the mirror
but it does not tick, tock;
instead, it whispers the seconds.

a world lays in front of me
orange and brown and red.
it turns, turns,
and sees me
eyes barely open
smile minimal but genuine.

the lips, the sheets, the hair
the skin that meets mine,
the juvenile sun,
the time,
the whisper —

everything is soft.

for the late nights

This is for the late nights.

The bedridden, lonely as can be, eternity stretched late nights.

Tonight has been a late night even before the sun fell this afternoon.

There's an empty space in your twin sized bed that makes you feel like even a royal family couldn't have a bed big enough for the one you're tossing and turning into. Your heart does not run in beats tonight; it cycles in the form of slurs with tempos that suspend on a constant measure of silence from questions in your head that will never be answered tonight.

It's a late night.

Your lips grind softly and you lick them well; yet you wonder why they're still dry. Your body holds its position in the most clinically comfortable way; yet there's a discomfort in the way your body holds nothing. You have a comforter over your legs accompanied by two sheets; but tonight of all nights — of many nights — you feel cold.

You're in love. You have someone to love.

But tonight is for the nights where you have everything — you even have a full heart — but tonight you also have nothing.

Because there is nothing that competes with the tranquility of laying with the calm beating of another's heart. With them, there is a fulfillment of space in your own central chamber of emotions. There is no comparison to the blanket of physical and emotional presence from existing with another human being that is zero miles away from your body.

Tonight is the night where you long for the moisture built of emotions which are exclusive to two people in a world of seven billion — the moisture that sits atop of one of the most intimate sensory organs that the human body possesses. Tonight you wrap your fingers around a body that your soul and heart both long for; but the only body you catch tonight is the empty space between the sheets. You are cold with an inflamed heart and a trembling soul.

You are in love; but tonight and tomorrow and the next day, it will be a long night while you long for the person that has the ability to make your night feel infinite.

72 degrees

things are different now
just as the seventy two degrees
that dance around
in the middle of december

but i will always love you
no matter the weather
even if the winter
fails to remember

oldschool

i can imagine
my last breath of life
still in love with you

but the future
will always have
secrets and surprises
to keep

but for now
i will reflect on the day
to every single night

and i will delightedly admit
that i am still in love with you
just as i fall asleep

distance

Monday:
Today I saw you.

I was paying for my groceries and you were the cashier three rows down. You were a girl engaged in conversation. I'm sure it was small talk which included your personal preference of the ripeness of various fruits or the best type of peanut butter. You had this grin on your face and a look in your eyes that would have made any customer pay extra just to get the chance to talk to you again. You then looked up, straight towards me, and your smile traveled faster through my heart than a ray of sunshine would have raced to the earth — even if it were the same distance of three grocery aisles away as we were.

Tuesday:
Today I heard you.

I attended a poetry reading at a small coffee shop in the outskirts of the city. I never liked reading poetry. Hell — I didn't even like looking at the readers as they read off of their notebooks. I held my cup of latte and opened my ears to anything that would catch my attention. There was a man that sounded like he was in his early twenties. When I heard the passion in his voice, I knew it was you. Every single word that bled out of your mouth had snaked its way into the skin of my chest and tattooed themselves to the base of my heart. I could feel the intensity of this blanket surround me, and when it was over, the warmth of your presence in my body took hours to dissipate back to normality.

Wednesday:

Today I felt you.

I was alone in my room. It was one of those days when the air was cold and the rain was wintery and so I had no desire to go outside. I missed you. It had been a month since I saw your face and heard your voice—that wasn't through a screen and speaker. I kept seeing you in the people I saw and the strangers I heard. When this would happen, I would look down at my hands and see my emotions form their own fingers and palms and I would swear that I could, once again, feel your body interlaced with mine. I would hear the wind whisper passion and intensity into my ears and I would swear that it was your whisper.

But until I see you again, my heart will beat and beat until the day your body reunites with your soul next to mine.

a thing about your bones

the reality
of falling in love
is that you will break
a couple or more bones

and if you land safely

then maybe
you did not

fall
    hard
        enough.

i woke up wanting to kiss you

There's a cough in my chest at twelve in the morning.

I'm in a moving car; the sky spins around me in linear paths. I'm looking at the stars tonight, wishing for a way to feel alive like I used to when I was with you.

There's a conversation going on between the wheels and the road. I can't hear what they say exactly; the conversations sputter in and out for my ears to grasp. I hear remnants of discussion wondering if I can make the drive home safely tonight.

I turn on the radio, and there's your voice. It's soft and warm with acoustic guitars dancing in the background. There's not much complexity in the lyrics. All I hear is your voice saying my name. I sing along perfectly, besides the fact that I'm not singing the correct lyrics — I'm just saying your name instead.

But somehow the lyrics rhyme; somehow the pitches match; somehow there's unison our breaths in and our cutouts.

When our song ends, so does the music. Nothing else comes on the radio — at least nothing that I can hear.

And so now I just sit here in whispers on the road — still singing our song and looking at the stars.

But I'm delusional.

I'm just sitting here in silence, muttering your name, and staring into a cloudy night.

21

i have found someone
that makes me realize
that raindrops do not always mean thunderstorms
and scratches do not always mean death

but i am sure
that when i am in my own storms
with arms scratched to death
she will be alongside me,
beating her heart
in my direction.

tails

in the distance
a dog with short, black hair
chases his own tail
as his owner laughs
through the record button

down the street
a child looks into
the clouded sky;
could it be the dinosaurs
or the lions or the sea ships
that the picture books
had always promised him?

even closer yet
a daffodil grows in a garden
and is hopeful that it can catch
the shadow that has been playfully
mocking it all day
the black has creeped closer to it for
the whole morning
it is 11:59 AM
the sun near the top

here now
an observationist could say
that I would be fucking idiotic
even if the observationist would be me

but after everything
I am in bliss;
my heart is enthralled;
even as I pursue nothing —
even as I chase you.

university of fear, dark thoughts

"Goodnight."
"Goodnight."

There is normally thirty minutes in between the silence of the end of the phone call and the last breath before you go to sleep. Most nights you spend this half our reflecting on your life—your life with her. You remember the moments spent with her. You think about the infinite possibilities of stories that will tattoo themselves onto the dimples of your brain. You recall the things she says. The jokes; the daily review of the day; or the intellectual responses that she supplies with your thinking mind.

Most of the time, you just sit and appreciate the presence she's had in your life. She's made you smile almost every night—just seconds before you enter your dreams just to meet her again.

"Goodnight."
"Goodnight."

Tonight, it's different. She didn't say much. She didn't talk about her day; she didn't mention the past memories; she didn't want to give you her thoughts. Goodnight is all the conversation is—and that hurts. It hurts because she is in pain and the only thing you can do is wonder *what happened, what went wrong, was it me, should I call back,* etc.

In the last thirty minutes the silent presence between you and her, these questions swirl around your neck and become tighter at each mark. The dimples on your cheeks from your smile now transform into wrinkles on your forehead.

You are devastated at the end of a conversation that ends mid-sentence. The silence of the night discomforts your soul and you feel broken.

But if you think like this, you are at an illusion. The questions that grip at your beating heart are not as detrimental as they seem. They blind you. They make you forget that she is still in your arms, even if she is silent; that her heart beats towards your direction; that she whispers your name in her prayers.

She is still in love with you. The only difference about tonight, and some nights to come, is that—for her— silence is more comforting than words. And by tomorrow, she will dive back into the waves of your sound.

"Good morning."
"Good morning."

for mondays

i know
that you wish
to not be on this earth
because it has been
the coldest winter
your bones have ever felt;

but i hope
that you have just
forgotten
that the warmth
will come again.

for all the fears

I am afraid that one day I will not be worth your time. I am afraid you will view our situation how everyone else will tell you when we first meet—that I am not the only one the only one in this world who acts like me, talks like me, and loves like me. There are those who are better and far more impressive than I am. And they will not live in some town far away that takes weeks at a time for us to see each other for just under 24 hours at a time.

I am afraid you will stop looking at me like your heart is beating out of your eyelids. I am afraid you will stop looking at me altogether. I am afraid that you will look at me and tell me you love me—just to feel the words articulate from your tongue; yet nothing will emote from your heart.

I am afraid that with your plans of succeeding in life, I will be left behind. I am afraid of being stranded in a city half as dense and a fraction as deep as the home that I have hollowed out in your heart. None of these things have happened—but all of these things might. I have become destroyed by my own decay and I am terrified of my own shadow and I don't want to lose you in the process of life. Right now my world spins like it always has. But tonight, I feel like I am in a tornado. I don't want to be dust.

sorry

No is your answer
with no remorse,
and no regrets —
not even
a single sliver of consideration.

I need to focus on one thing at a time you say,
as you look forward
and I lay behind
knowing that you can feel
the aching tremors of my heart.

Sorry,
as you turn
the other way.

hiatus,

i have suffocated
in the discomfort of
an indefinite duration
between the dialogue of your

"i..."
and

"...love you"
or
"...can't do this"

and i am left
in a hiatus,

US,
AND
THEN
THERE
WAS

our final song

I've never listened to song lyrics — not attentively, at least. I've learned the words to some — the radio will overplay them like that — but I've never actually listened to songs to the extent where the meaning has seeped into my bloodstream. In some ways, I believe it is habitual.

I grew up around sisters that played the piano; I myself played the violin in my childhood. My ears were trained instrumentally even as I grew older. Entering my adolescence, I signed up for band class. I was taught to listen for balance between the lows and highs of the instrumentation. I had to listen for the tone and intonation for individuals as well as in the group as a whole. I had to stay aware of my articulations and where each type was deemed appropriated. And most of all, I learned that without meaning — without emotion — the song would mean nothing to the instrumentalist.

I was trained all of these things in a world where half of the songs in the world had lyrics to go along with the music. There was human emotion in instrumental music — that's what made it music in the first place. But words, language, communication — that was the basis of humanity itself.

I discovered this second half of the world when I met her. She was a vocalist her whole life. She sang everywhere, at all times, no matter the circumstance. I, as someone who created music externally from my fingers, lungs, and tongue, watched her as music slipped from her mouth; not from tone, pitch, or articulation — but through her words.

"You're so awkward, and I love that" was one of the first songs of this new world that I was only just beginning to discover. Soon enough, "I love you" became one of my favorites. She tried not to play it too frequently, but I didn't blame her if she did. It was catchy; not because it flowed easily off the tongue, but because it cannonballed straight into my soul. I wasn't the first person to whom this song was sung, but every time I listened to her sing it, I was her only audience.

Some of the songs she sang were originals—I was the first person that had ever heard these lyrics. Not every song was as pretty as the hit that had captivated me to keep listening, but every song had depth. Every lyric had meaning—whether it were drawn from the clouds or inked by a bleeding soul. Any direction the songs traveled, I cherished her lyrics. To me, the instrumentals of her whispers meant significantly less if her words were the ones that screamed.

Months passed. I had listened to her entire discography at that point—the ones that she gave me, at least. "I love you" began to play repetitively—and just as my natural instincts were taught, I began listening to the instrumentals of the background music. It turned into comfort music; the type that I listened to as I washed the dishes instead of the music that I painted murals to. The song turned into a radio-edited version; its whispered instrumentals converted into a sped up, electronic party mix. It was a feel-good moment to hear the song—but only for a minute before the euphoria died away. It used to be a song that I would spend nights of wondering about its intricacies and layers; but now, it was just a pop song that overplayed itself into the normality of life.

The day came where she no longer wanted to sing the song anymore. There was a song for that, too. I heard the lyrics but chose not to listen to the words despite the weight that they carried with them.

The dynamics were a mezzo piano for the most part. The attacks of her articulations were strong at first, but they quickly died at the ends of each phrase. The tone of her voice was treacherous; it trembled uncontrollably. But the emotion — it was there. It was definitely there.

I hopped into her car. She had to drive me back home, where I would never hear another live performance from her again — at least I would never hear "I love you" ever again. I realized this as she shut the car door.

We pulled out of the driveway when she turned on the radio. A song began. Its instrumentation consisted of a single guitar; acoustic. The legato plucking of the strings were the instrumentation before the lyrics began. Thirty four beats of this guitar's melody played before the lyrics began; the tears started rolling down my face by the end of the first measure.

The song was about love. The lyrics were about two people that had met for the very first time.

And here I was, crying, at the end of our very own song.

I still don't listen to song lyrics much. But maybe I should, all the time. I might miss something important, just as I did with her. Silence isn't as great of a song as hers were to me. With silence, everything is instrumentally perfect; the balance and blend, tone, intonation — it's all correct. But it has no words. It has no emotion. It has none of her.

364 nights

364 nights i have gone to sleep,
reading your name on the backs of my eyelids,
riding its pronunciation on the grooves of my lips,
smelling syllables on sweatshirts that i have not
washed since February.

364 nights i have taken eyes hidden behind
the glares of glass for granted (an
aperture that sees more life than most),
with irises like the ocean
on days when people do not go outside —
only you do.

364 nights i have said your name
and i have always traveled to the future,
my name always coming back to me
for 364 nights in a row

but 365
i will only find the past.

dmitri

a composer
created a piece six years later
to honor his late wife
and i wonder
if i will still be writing poetry
about the skeleton flowers
and the deceased imprints
that you have left on my soul

you are not dead
but you have left a presence
that has collapsed
inside of my syllables
and i am just spitting
out rot

the beginning

The end.

Yesterday you seemed out of it. You walked with me; however, you did not smile like you always had—you hadn't in a while, actually. But yesterday you did not even give a single attempt to perform any measurement of happiness. I soon found out what those silences meant; what the reasons were for the bags under your eyes. What spoke from those avoiding eyes.

A couple of months ago, you told me that you felt that we were comfortable around each other. I had already heard that from you three or four times; but this time, it you sounded like you feared this comfortability. I tried not to think about it; but then I found myself taking trips around my twin-sized bed, eyes forcefully clenched in frustration. I did not know what you meant by this. *Find the answers, find the answers, find the —*

Half a year ago, you kept poking me in my sides because you knew I was ticklish there, just as I was in every other body part. You began to call me nicknames from movies that we watched, different songs that we would slow dance to when you visited my home for the first time, and from the different foods we both enjoyed. You looked at me like this could be something worth your time. You looked at me and I knew you loved me.

Nine months ago, we ran into each other in the hallway. I had just transferred into your school—which was rare, considering the fact that I only had a year left until college. You were one of the first people I met—or at least one of the first people that I met that was worth remembering. I was shy; I hadn't made any close friends since I started middle school. It was a good thing you were welcoming—or maybe you were just talkative. But I knew when I met you—or at least I hoped to the final point of my heart—that you were going to be a main character in some of the important stories of my life.

This is how I met you. This was our beginning:

7 billion

it is true:
i am young and the world is at my fingertips
and i have so much more to give to it
but on some hours my skin wrinkles when i cry
like i am the elderly who is the first to die of his family
and i do not understand loss
and my fingers grow weary
to the point where i grasp the air of my hands
and the weight of gravity is too heavy
and i will give everything i have
to seven billion people compiled on this earth
but i will give nothing
because i only know how to give everything
to one single person
worth my entire world

bad timing

You and I were together when Bad Timing introduced itself into our lives. As time went on, we became more and more familiar with the type of image that Bad Timing placed on us. Eventually, we decided to trust anything it told us, even if the things it told us to do conflicted with me and you.

It came to the point where Bad Timing became better friends with us individually than what we were with each other. When that moment came, it told one of us to walk away and the other to keep together. And so between you and me, our relationship became a game of chasing and stabbing each other's hearts—and it was okay—because of Bad Timing.

It was okay to ignore every paragraph filled with pleads of the past, even if every word was true to your heart. Bad Timing said there was no way that a single letter was true, no matter the length.

It was okay to touch the lips of ones that you didn't actually love, even if you still felt the heartbeat of the person from so long ago. Bad timing said that, in life, a heartbeat will eventually stop, including the one that occupied yours.

It was okay to not believe any emotion that made you feel like you were lonely even if your mind begged your body to feel that way. Bad Timing always made it apparent that everything the other person said was the right thing—because that's what Bad Timing told them.

You and I were together when Bad Timing introduced itself into our lives. But we became so accustomed to the idea of it that it brought us apart, broke us, and started an emotional fire. But we chose that to happen to us. We chose to put the responsibility of our relationship into an inconvenience of time.

Bad timing happens, but it shouldn't have been an excuse to treat one another like shit. If we're going to say that you and I are not on good terms because of bad timing, then we are wrong. All we did was turn an unfortunately-timed situation into a worse situation. And no matter what direction we will face, one of us willingly will look away, while the other will stare straight into the other's eyes because of the manipulation of Bad Timing. Because of us.

goodbye

there is nothing good about goodbyes,
especially not when my tears flow
down the skin of my face:
the one you've always kissed
on mornings
when you had to drive back home.

there is nothing good about goodbyes,
when i expect to hear a good hello
but it never enters my ears:
the ones that
i love you and *we'll be okay*
used to enter so frequently.

there is nothing good about goodbyes,
not anymore,
after all:
you use it in past tense now

goodbye,
and there i go,
and there you go:

goodbyed.

ours

This is where it ends; this is where all things turn relative. This is where pain is just a feeling, a heart is just a beating, the sky is just a falling. This is where the songs aren't Ours, they're just songs. The restaurants are just restaurants, our wrists are just bare, our fingers are just empty. This is where the mornings aren't soft and the nights aren't having a good sleep; they're just when the sun comes up and falls back down. This is where the dreams don't mean shit; they're just dreams, they're just memories; memories that aren't about Us—they're just about you thinking about Us and what we used to be. Even the thoughts of us in the future are made up of memories. This is where you let Us go, although Us does not acknowledge it and Us never will; Us will live forever in love even if you never come back, even if you go away, find another Us—one that consists of not you and her. This is where you stop, this is where it ends, this is where it dies, this is where it resurrects to our memories, this is where we forget, this is where we get up, this is where we walk away, this is where you don't look back—this is where you look back anyway. This is where you look back, look up, at the sky, and you see the sunset. This is where you tell yourself that they're just colors and colors don't mean shit. This is where you can't help but for a moment disagree. This is where you know that she, Us, you, know—that these are not colors. This is where you know that somewhere, the sunset is still Ours. Maybe not in this world, maybe not in this dimension, but maybe, maybe, maybe:

This is where Ours lives on.

under the sky

the sky is just the sky,
blue and empty and carefree,
gray and dark and somber,
yellow and orange and pink of emotion,
and somewhere you are under it,
and somehow i think of you
while looking up.
but it is just the sky,
and you do not notice me at all.

broken gravity

I—I do not know where or when things started to go wrong. I remember the times when there was no other choice than the route to go up—a route that others perceived as insanity, but a direction where we knew happiness awaited.

We found exactly what we were looking for while others scratched their heads and frowned to the skies as they looked at two people; up too high, heading too fast, and loving way too young. We penetrated through the clouds without much interference. Where most couples would find turbulence, lose balance, and in result, crumble, crack, and be forced to land back to the ground, our heads were sharp. We sliced through the earliest stages of bumps and bruises that we were aware of enduring.

One time, I decided to turn around, and I saw the world behind us. The rounded horizon of the sunset illuminated the places we conquered together. I turned around and we shot higher into the atmosphere, almost indestructible and ready for anything. We exited the ozone layer and began the exploration of space.

However, one night, as we accelerated through the galaxy, rocks began hitting our bodies. There were pebbles and dust that had scraped us before, but not like this. Boulders, jagged and sharp, began denting the sides of our defenses. We had run into debris. By the end of it, you became more damaged than me—but still we were intact. Still we were together as one. We escaped with rocks and dirt between us, but they would eventually brush off. We suddenly aged far older than what most couples would have at this point. But we were still there.

But later, as I turned around to see the pale blue dot of earth, I turned around, and you were gone. Half of us was gone. I began to suffocate uncontrollably, my skin expanding, my heart exploding, instantly—for you had disappeared without prior notice. I felt no creaking or cracking or stripping of your presence from my own. In seconds I was destroyed.

Usually, one can feel when they lose projection. They can feel the direction go from up to down. But I could not feel that. We went up, and we were destroyed. Obliterated. Perhaps we did not go into space; perhaps we were in the ocean. Not going up; but always heading down to the ocean floor. And here I was, alone at rock bottom.

wisdom teeth

my breath smells so much like shit
and i hate how the oxycodone
makes the world vibrate like something
good is finally going to happen
but i always wake up and it's 2PM
and then it's three in the morning
and i'm sweating in bed
itching in all the skin where
you used to touch me
but you're not home with me at all
and i'm just stuck in a world
before i met you and one after
and the medicine tears me apart
as i look at all of these memories
not knowing if i was a part of them
at all and i miss you

dreammare

i do not cling to my bed sheets
at nine to ten to eleven am
because i would rather close my eyes
in a world where i can experience
the complexity of a life that is complete;
but because there is a universe,
although a parallel,
there is one that exists nonetheless
where i close my eyelids
and you are still there.

walled

How easy must it be to speak to a brick wall; you may say what you want or none at all and you will gain the same effect: nothing and nothing.

It is much less of a gamble to talk to an infrastructure held together by hardened concrete that is painted over and over by coats of protection and is set into the softness of the earth. It does not react at all to a word you say. It does not feel happiness or sadness or madness or jealousy. It does not feel vanity for your wildly profound possessions or empathy for your cursed wounds. It does not hug you when you are withered or bite you when it feels threatened. It is there and you may draw what you want to see in front of you; a sky, a hole, a shadow, or a stick figure to keep you company so it may have conversation with you so that you feel like you create a relevant presence.

How beautiful must that feel to have that control? How beautiful must it feel to smile at a brick wall that can easily be manipulated with a crayon and some creativity to smile directly back; to pretend that things are okay?

But now that there is a brick wall in between us, do I even dare even speak? It is so easy for me to love a brick wall. It is so easy to talk to a brick wall even though it will not speak back; even though my stick figures do not move; even though the illustrations mock me with their jagged grins and slanted eyes.

But I must do it anyway, because I know you are somewhere on the other side. And I am inches away from it. But you are miles and miles away and you do not look back. Your hands are coated in the mud that has formed the division that slices open my heart and lies on both sides. Why do you even speak back as if you are speaking to a wall of hardened earth?

no apologies for the broken heart

i'm sorry you can't look me in the eyes anymore
if they even mean a goddamned thing
they're black and dark and everything
you'd want to avoid *before getting hurt*

i can't imagine how it feels like
to stare into the night
in the middle of the day
but your eyes are blue
blue like the sky that is beautiful
and the oceans that are tranquil
and when i open my own
you are everywhere
and it hurts when it is sunny and beautiful
when the world tells me
it is well for me again
and i cannot agree

because this world is not you
the sky is just overcast
the water is just muddy
my eyes are just gray

5:45 in the morning

things have been going quite well if i say so myself
the green in us has eventually crowned into white petals
and it feels beautiful and she can agree
with my silly flower analogies
just to laugh at (or with)
and i agree with her myself
and i do not care at all
and i care all the many

but then one day
a petal falls on the ground
and she realizes it and i tell her it's ok
it's ok, it's o k
but she does not hear me or feel me or see me
her thoughts scream too loud

there's a white petal on the fucking ground
we're not even that high up!
but she cannot believe that we have lost ((one))
I loved you she says
I love you not

it was just a metaphor!
i'm pleading now.
it's not beautiful to her anymore.
we've lost.

we're just a fucking weed.

i'm okay, no i'm not

You don't know what you've lost. You take a smile and you pretend that it's okay. That when you go about your day you have a good fucking day even it's a pretend fucking day. A good conversation even if it's a pretend conversation. You don't want it to hurt, so you don't go to the hurt. For your reasons, I am in your hurt, so you don't go to me anymore.

One day you came to me after sleeping in the same bed and you said, "I don't want to hurt you anymore."

You could have just said you didn't want to hurt yourself anymore by being with me. You could have just cut my neck then and there, but you didn't. Because it is a pretend game from here. You say that this is just you, that you need time away; but you tell me, when you sip your poison and stare into the eyes of someone else that it is okay — even as you pretend.

This is where we disagree. I can never pretend. I can never ignore. I can never be okay when I'm not. You have picked me up and left me in the hurt, and I have stayed here for months trying to figure out why you have left me here. Meanwhile, you must pretend that it's okay. You must pretend that *it's okay it's okay it's okay* and suddenly, you are fucking okay, suddenly you are fucking moved on, suddenly you are with someone else, doing other things, *being happy, being happy, being happy, being happy* — and I am just in the fucking hurt waiting for you to come the fuck home — and why are you not fucking home?

You tease me and say I love you too when I am telling the truth and I miss you too when I'm hanging upside down, take me out of the hurt, take me fucking out — because I cannot pretend like you can.

-

( )

fuck (you)
i hate circles
more than i ever wanted to now
and i'm tempted
to not recycle anymore
because it reminds me
of (you) the sprints
i had to take from
old to new to knew to (you)
then just me.

If this were parenthetical,
i bet (you) the lines wouldn't
even read my eyes.
(you) this poem doesn't make sense—
only parts of it does.

But if this poem were me,
parenthetically,
i would leave the ends open,
and cycle back to (you

subliminal

things have never been so subliminal
hello means *i love you* means
just *hello* again.

okay is the hands that massage the shoulders
is the grip that tenses the body

a smile for us
is for just me then
is for only you now

am i all in my head
when i see circles
as you speak in straight lines?

in the trash bin

It is a strange thing to be the one who is thrown away. You begin to wonder where you stand — or if you can even stand at all — since your mind is crumpled and your heart is torn. A striking realization begins to tell you that you are as delicate and weak as a single sheet of paper; however, many memories ago, you were as thick as a trunk.

You look around you, in this bin of all these things that have been thrown away before. You have no idea who or what these things are, other than the stories that have been told that have created them. Past loves. Past friendships. Past memories. It is peculiar because now you are down here with all of them.

Now you are one of them; a lifeless object in someone else's wasteland. At this point you have accepted that there is no going back — if you are to be unfolded, you will just be a damaged product of what you used to mean. So you sit here and hibernate in this forgotten file inside of this dusty, neglected shelf.

There is nothing at all that you can control in this situation; there is nothing you can change. You may hibernate here for years — possibly even forever — and there is no way of knowing the duration. Not until they say so. But somewhere in this dimming memory — which pulsates less and less every day now — you wish that you were thrown into a recycling bin instead of a trash can. And maybe you have been. But for now, you are still crumpled. You are still here.

dandelions

I know you are just waiting for the
wind to pick you up
and I swear that I love dandelions too

but I am a goddamned paper clip
and all I am is weight
all I am meant to do is wait

and for some reason
I have attached myself to you
I'm so sorry the world has to
switch gravities for me to
let you go.

—4:15 A.M.

"You're here again," she said, laying still, facing the cracks of the window.

"It seems so."

It was raining delicately. Things were finally cooling down—their body temperatures, their heart rates, and even the bed sheets. So was the conversation.

"It feels different," he whispered. "Why won't you say anything? Why won't you give me any more advice?"

He had his hands around her hips. They were lace, just like the curtains which he faced.

There was a silence that could have been awkward between the two, but it wasn't. They were too close—too comfortable—to feel uneasy about their responses.

"You know, your breath really smells like shit right now," she said in a raspy tone, chuckling along in the process.

He didn't respond.

She turned her torso to face him.

Not even his face had a reaction.

"What?" she asked. "It's true."

"Are you not gonna answer my questions?"

He sounded agitated.

"Besides . . . your breath smells like my—"

"Your what??" she interjected, poking him in the side, before the two burst into laughter, lightened their faces, and kissed.

"I love you," he whispered in his exhale.

Immediately—and almost regretfully—she turned back at the window. The smile from both of their faces dissipated instantly. There was another silence; although this time, a silent chord struck from the paucity of dialogue.

"No you don't."

The boy backed from her body although he never moved an inch in any direction. He just stared at the back of her head. With his eyes, he followed the continuous lines of her shadowed hair down her backside. He didn't know what to think.

"I don't?"

"No."

For a while, they laid there in the bed, his hands on her laced hips, her body tightly packed into the embracement of his, together, yet separated.

She would sniffle occasionally — then, in a miniscule fashion, would periodically shift a leg or an arm through the sandwiched sheets. He sat still, taking every auditory detail of the room as an explanation for why she said the things that she just did.

She finally summoned enough courage to tell him what was on her mind.

"You don't love me, babe. At least — you're not supposed to."

She felt him nod behind her, but she wasn't sure if it was a nod of agreement or denial.

"I'm . . . seeing someone else."

He wasn't surprised by this. He wasn't hurt either — at least not initially. He still didn't have a response for her words. The things she said were more than just words — they were more than just actions. Everything that came out her mouth from the minute they met shot a significant blow to the boy's direction in life. A single word could mend his thousand-piece puzzle of a heart in a minute. The same one could bat it to pieces in a second. Right now, he didn't prefer either option.

"Who?"

"You don't know him. But he's wonderful. He makes me happy."

"That's good. I'm happy for you."

His response suspended to the fan above them. Both of them could feel its weight pulling their individual hearts apart. She took her hands up from underneath the covers and ran her fingers behind her along the side of his left leg. There was a sulking weight on her face as she looked at the particles of light captured inside the raindrops.

"You know . . . I still think about you from time to time," she whispered.

"I know. That's why we're both still here."

He ran his own fingers down her leg this time, and right under her knee, slowed down.

She smiled.

"Don't you dare."

"Stop. Stop!!"

He tickled her in one of her only sensitive spots on her body. They laughed at each other again as their bodies coincided in their own warmth.

"You know, I was so happy when I was with you," he said, with a smile still streaked across his face.

"I was, too. At least until the end."

Her smile diminished slightly as she thought back to the darker part of her memories. The two didn't need an explanation for why their laughs kept dying so quickly. It was an unfortunate ending. But it had to happen for the both of them.

"Babe . . ."

"Yes?"

"He's going to take me to the top of that hilltop tomorrow—you know, the one with the cemetery? And he's going to tell me he loves me. I'm finally going to forget about you."

He was struck. He swallowed the tongue inside his throat. For a moment, he knew that he couldn't think about it forever. As much as he didn't want it to happen, he knew this was going to come eventually.

"What's going to happen to us? Here, I mean."

She sniffled, this time, out of sadness.

"I don't know. I may never come back," she said.

"But don't you miss it? This?" He was pleading now.

"Yes. I'm here for a reason, babe. But I won't—not after tomorrow."

He sighed. It was the end. The last ever; the final credits; the light at the end of the day. He held her tighter in the bed, knowing that he would never be able to anymore from this moment on.

She turned over to look at him, her whole body facing him now. She ran her fingers along the side of his face.

"I'm sorry," she whispered.

"Don't apologize," he said, eyes downward, as he slid his fingers into hers. "I know it's been a while, but I never forget what happens next."

"I hope you know that I never like doing this," she said, as tears formed in her eyelids. "I'm so sorry babe."

"It's okay. It really is," he said, as he closed his eyes.

She got out of the sheets on her side of the bed, reached for the pistol on the side table, checked the cartridge, and cocked it. She looked out the window; to the raindrops; through the laced curtain. There were tears strolling down her face as if she turned into the window itself as if she became the mirror this time.

He saw her backside. Her hair illuminated the monochromatic room of the night. His eyes followed the lines as they flowed gracefully down her neck. Finally, they trickled to a stop halfway down her bare back. His eyes kept going, finding the lace. It was torn now. He sighed, then smiled.

"Let me see you, babygirl. One last time."

She stood up, her body trembling. It was cold in the room, but not cold enough to shake like she was.

"God damn. You're beautiful."

She didn't say a word. She was on the brink of bursting into an amount of tears that could drown the entire room. But she couldn't do that to him. Especially not now. Not in this last time.

He didn't smile. But he wasn't frowning either.

She pulled up the pistol and aimed it straight into his heart, irons directly on sight.

"I . . . still love you. I know it's the wrong time to say this. But it's the last time I can ever tell you. Even if you will never actually hear it for yourself. I want you to know that I still do, even when you forget about me tomorrow. I love you."

She gasped, unable to contain the strike that the boy's words blew onto her heart.

This isn't him, she pleaded to herself.

But what if it was? What if it still is?

A waterfall from her face eased through her shaking fingers.

"I . . . I . . . can't."

"I know babygirl. You just have to pull the tri—"

Pop! Pop! Pop!

. . .

—8:37 A.M.

He shot up from his covers, gasping for air. "Fuck."

He rolled out of bed delicately. Morning wood.

Stumbling around the bed to the window across his room, he acknowledged the lace curtains. He tore them down, irritated at the stupidity of the suspension that it created in the room just from something as light as the air. He looked at the window. It was drying up outside. So was he.

. . .

—9:26 A.M.

She woke with trembling hands. As soon as she opened her eyes, the tears began exiting her ducts. She looked around a distorted room as if she were underwater. Her throat was already gallons under before coughing her emotions back into stability.

She felt arms quickly wrap around her torso from behind her.

"Hey, hey, hey now, it's okay... you're okay...I'm here babe. You're okay. You're safe," her boyfriend urgently said in an attempt to alleviate her impromptu outcry.

His breath smelled.

Hers did too.

"We have a day planned," her boyfriend said, smiling.

She said nothing.

"We're going to the best view of the city. Are you ready? I'll make some breakfast."

The boyfriend climbed out of bed groggily, walked to the door, and closed it softly.

She stared at the ceiling as she adjusted her lace.

She and her boyfriend were going to the cemetery today.

She and the boy were already there.

nine.

i apologize, for
there is a disruption in my words
as it feels as if tape has ducked my lips
and i have been kidnapped into a cave
miles into the darkness
with my mouth facing away from the light.

i apologize, for
my ears hear your rejoice in freedom
but never have i heard my own chords
plead so much in oppression.

i apologize, for
it feels like i have not spoken my mind
but grains of salt
grind my beating organs
when i realize that i have already cut my piece

and you
have just not taken it

i love you elisabethsomuch

You never come out of a heartbreak refreshed; that is, if it meant anything to you at all. There's a reason it has taken you a long duration until people start to turn heads and ask you, "Honey, are you okay?"

They call you honey because it's not your friends who notice your shambled pace of life. It's the adults who express their concerns because they went through the things you are going through right now—things your friends haven't felt yet.

There's a reason it's taken you this long to finally feel comfortable by yourself because at one point, you looked across the table at the diner when the rain began falling like it was autumn again and you told yourself, "Fuck the world. They are my world now."

And then you blinked down, then back up, and they just stayed at you, laughing and wondering why you were blinking in the first place.

But you knew this was a risk. You were sixteen. You didn't know shit. But you did know love. You knew it through the hickies on your neck; through the batting heartbeats; through the clenched fists from the arguments. Through sickness and health. Through death.

And now death has come and killed that part of you, buried it, and put a shitty wooden memorial on top that's already rotting on the grave. And you have to act like you don't give a fuck about the past—whether it was good or bad—just so it doesn't get worse.

And then you grow older. And you find someone else, even though you're shy and they're twice as shy as you, so you just stand around them at the end of the class, hoping that they appreciate your willing presence. And then you forget about this heartbreak from about seven in the morning to seven in the night.

But now, you're thinking about it. And you're still halfway not giving a shit. But you think about it really hard, for just a moment. And you realize something that you forgot to realize before you stopped caring:

The heartbreak was always worth it. Because love, whether it ends in a shootout, or in a handshake agreement, is always worth it. They were always worth it. You were.

But for now, you're here. And you can't tell them — they're already gone. But if you throw the thought into the sky, the air that will take your whispering prayers will give you closure. And eventually, it does.

,

this is me,
breathing in,
breathing out,
feeling no, air,
pass through, my lungs,
feeling no, release, from the,
weight of my, chest,
feeling, no end to any thought,
at all,
somaybeifitalkallatonceallatthesametime,
i,
    will,
        stop,
            thinking,
about the millions, of speculations,
that my self-depre, cating, head,
throws, at my heart,
andiwillrunoutofthingstohurtme,
andi'll,
    just,
        runoutof,
            breath,

never forget this, part two

536 Days Later

If you ever forget (which — my god, if you ever forget):

Remember her eyes. They're the first and last thing that you knew about her. Some nights, they still find themselves in your bed from the dreams. Every morning, they will definitely still be there — at least for a while. They say the eyes are windows, and your memory of her is right behind that pane of transparency.

Remember her voice. Remember the voicemails through the distorted gates of the telephone. Remember the way her whispers snuck into your memories like warmth does on chilly nights. Remember the way her laugh clipped onto your cheeks and lifted them to happiness. The voice is the vehicle of every thought, prayer, and question that she has ever planted into your mind. Remember that there are trees inside of you because of her voice.

Remember her lips. They kissed you like how your own trembled in awe of how fast time passed when an ounce is added to the formula of life. Remember how they filled the cracks of your broken heart as you felt like drowning in the saline tears that met her own face. Remember how she made you feel as if the tears were not yours; instead, *ours.* Remember how they arched into a hint of hope — for her more than you — before she said, "We'll see each other again. I'm sure of it."
Her lips are the ones to remember for all the highs she helped you through and all the lows that she pushed you to endure.

There was a time where, if you had ever forgotten these things, life would be pass or fail; but forgetting these things now can be as mindless as burning wood to keep a fire going or taking out the trash to provide more space. Remembering these things about her have reached nullification. They are as neutral as the color of gray when it is placed next to a sunset that bleeds the death of its day. In fact, you shouldn't remember her by these things.

Remember her eyes as the ones that blink at the thought of a past with accompanied with the denial of its legitimacy. Remember the way they pointed towards the ground while intentionally knowing that your own were drowning for her attention. Remember that eyes are windows but they can also be mirrors — and when she looks at you (and what *us* used to be), her eyes will turn as the black as the emptiness that rests in her archives. Remember her voice as the one that said "I can't," after saying "I hope this will last forever." You knew you were young; but at the time, you believed her because *she* believed her, even after she admitted that she lied. Remember her voice in the phone call — after you couldn't take one more voicemail — when she said, "The guy I'm with now is so great."

Remember that she used the same exact voice to tell her ex before you the same exact thing — except back then, you were "The Guy I'm With Now." Remember that there is only one voice per person, but they can create completely different masks. Remember that at one point, she wore the mask that loved you. Remember that now, she wears the mask doesn't anymore.

Remember her lips as the ones dosed in your tears after ending it swiftly. Remember how she kissed you the night before with the same purity as when things were suspended on pillars of love — yet only this time, she knew that things were upon the edges of her flames. Remember her voice fading away as she said goodbye with a fabricated hope — knowing that her goodbye was final.

If you ever forget these things, you'll remember the things you exercised yourself to remember for years. You'll remember the glass before she shattered it. You'll remember the forests that grew with you before they burned. You'll remember the highs and lows before the tracks of the roller coaster combusted into oblivion. You'll remember her soul the most — this beautiful mosaic of every compiled emotion you've ever felt tied with every memory of the past and vision every vision for the future. You'll remember and fall in love with her soul again. You'll fall in love with both concepts of the past and the future, and you won't be able to tell a difference. If you forget these things, you will fall in love with a false image. It is easier to make things up and convince your emotions to apply themselves than it is to fill the holes inside of you that she made with bits and pieces of your old memories and recite her name in poetry than it is to understand that emptiness takes up no space in between four walls.

So remember her.

But also remember the void that she created with the same eyes that introduced, the same voice that whispered, and the same lips that promised you forever.

joel

strange,
how we are so far
from one another now;
that my memories are
just metaphors
of what they used to be.

you'll find my poetry collection
and laugh
because you'll know
i've scooped my pieces
from the recycling bin.

but i only go dumpster diving
on occasion now,
and it still smells like you
of all things,
at least i think it does
unless it is just the metaphor

of you

thunderstorms

When you were mine, I used to love everything about summer thunderstorms.

I remember looking up into 4:37 PM skies, feeling the heat plaster across my face and seeing an ever-transitioning mural that formed among the clouds. Following close behind was grey matter that kept our history contained within a monotone shade. If I weren't with you, it'd probably look ominous.

The way you whispered your secrets into my ears provided the same effect as hearing thunder for the first time; a calming tone before the actual storm came.

The way you'd look into my eyes—a slight sparkle here and there—was coincidentally similar to seeing the first streaks of pleasurable lightning bolts I'd see right before the storm cloud was above my head.

And at this point, the temperature of the air—just like the temperature of my body—was nearly at a breaking point to where the earth begged for precipitation just as I thirstily awaited the moisture of your lips.

The storm, in both the sky and from your heart, always arrived at the same time of the day.

I loved everything about summer thunderstorms; every rain drop; every rolling cloud; every afterwards smell of the remaining ozone layer. It never got old frankly because of the way your heart pulsed to the extremity of the thunderstorm. I loved the fact that every day I'd feel the beating pulse of beautiful chaos against my own storm.

But I knew you grew tired of being just a summer thunderstorm every day. I knew you were tired of everything we were. And so you left.

And now the summer storms are back, and all I ever hear is your laugh in the thunder. All I ever see is your smile in the lightning veins. All I ever crave is the texture of your lips.

You'll always be a thunderstorm to me. But you're not the same one that I used to run into. You're chaos without being beautiful, and all I can do is long for a heart that will no longer be mine.

All I can do is sit in a summer thunderstorm that will never fucking end.

you're always in my blood, boiling

i was not lying
when i said you were the one
like how husbands do
at the funeral
or when dogs howl
in the rest home
or how children decide
in elementary

but winter has already
come and gone
you have died and resurrected
and i have found new
tails to chase
we have found youth again
but you nor i do not
exist in one another

for you
are still the one
who got away.

the window seat

I longed for the window seat every time I traveled by plane. Even as a grown man, I would still stare outside the layered glass to watch the earth shrink below me. When everyone else would take a brief glance out of the curved rectangle, shut the flap, and nod off to sleep, the children passengers—and I—would still be in awe of the ever-changing scenery of the world. The curiosity of this angle kept me from shutting eye to an earth that I had known for decades; however, this was a version that still surprised me with every chance I took to be in the sky.

When we met, my neck was in the clouds; however, her presence was enough for me to look through the white wisps of sky that surrounded me. Her eyes were the color of the horizons that I was so used to. Her voice was the sound of the ordinary, tranquil whispers that wrapped themselves around the levitating container I had always sat in. And finally—most importantly—the turbulence that she gave me kept me guessing if I were passing above the clouds or down to the earth.

She was like every experience I had while in the sky; but then, she wasn't. She was a sky that belonged to the world, just as I did; just as the clouds and the blues and the colds. But simultaneously, she was an atmosphere that was above the ozone layer—one that didn't freeze or suffocate me. She was the sky herself; a plane to me; an object too far above the earth for everyone else.

So when she said she loved the window seat, I let her. I sat in the middle seat next to her—and it was okay. I didn't have to look out of the window to see the sky. My sky. The same one that I had been observing for years; except that it wasn't. It was her now. And I was in love.

It had been a couple years later when she was still sitting at the window seat; I, still away from it, admiring her. But I wasn't staring at the skies anymore. They were just her. I peeked over her shoulder and looked out of the glassed window for the first time in years, and I noticed that we were on the ground. I didn't know how long we'd been there. I didn't feel the wheels hit the ground; maybe it had been while I was asleep. Maybe we had landed a year ago; I didn't know. I began sweating. I couldn't do it anymore. There was more to my world than her; but I had forgotten all of it and capped a filter over my eyes; her.

That's how I knew we couldn't grow anymore; for we were just staring into the ground when there were wings grown into my back. I had to fly again. I had to see the clouds; but not if she was in the way.

flowers still bloom in the summer

flowers still bloom in the summer
at least i think i hope they do
at least that is the only thing i remember

i know you did not want me to pick you
from your roots
although you were beautiful
i could not be the earth
that gives you life

but it was june
and our soil shriveled into dust
and although you were beautiful
you were dying
even if only through the stems

and you picked me
if not for beauty
if not for materialism
but for desperation

you picked me
without knowing that
in september it rains
in winter it rains
in spring it rains

so when it is april
you will still be planted in the garden bed
and although you are beautiful
i will not be there to know

four

for a moment i saw the sun;
warmth extended throughout my droughted bones
and there was normality, finally,
in the face of my heart.

the next time i blinked,
my eyes burned into the extremities
of the darkness
and before me was the night

for i had stared far too long into the black
waiting for the sun to shine on me once again
as i cried into the reflection of the moon.

nostalgia

There's nothing between us anymore. Everything bad has come — and then has become resolved. Every heartbreak we've ever shared will never happen again. Every fight; every argument; every single glare that we will shoot at each other will never have an impact on our hearts like the way it once used to.

Because we've decided to go separate directions, and finally it has ended on good terms.

That's what we say.

That's what we think.

That's what we hope for.

But it won't happen.

Because even after all of these things have happened to us, you're still not used to change. You're not used to difference. You're not used to emptiness. You're not used to being free. It's the harsh truth, for both of us.

Because when my mind speaks a little loud for my heart's capacity with phrases that include "No longer loving you," and "Nothing in between us," it doesn't just refer to the burdens of arguments, or the struggles of honesty, or the tensions of self-respect.

It also means that I'll never be welcomed by a smile that wraps around my soul. It means that I'll never be able to say goodnight at three am on random weekdays. It means that I'll never be able to brush your hand in the hallway — sometimes unintentionally, but always comforting. I won't be able to be mad at you for no apparent reason. And at the same expense, I won't be able to be in love with you for all of the obvious reasons.

There comes a time where you have to weigh if it's worth sharing the hate and love with someone constantly — or if it's worth it to not feel a thing at all.

So why does it hurt when you say you do not love me?

Why does it hurt the most—when you say you no longer hate me?

beautiful, blind

You've got beautiful eyes.
Ones that people usually refrain from complimenting
until they are comfortable enough to say
without being strange (but if i were honest,
i have had these thoughts from the start);
ones that laugh at sarcasm
even if i were trying
and ones that flicker
out of car windows
and ones that look away
even when it is
just the silence that is awkward.

You've got eyes
that will subdivide my thoughts
and transpose them into poetry
and i will write about them
if i can
and i am not writing about them
at all
and to my eyes, your eyes are
beautiful
and; but—

your heart is blind.

about the eclipse

"Hi."

He sounded timid.

"You look beautiful tonight."

It was still early when the moon mustered up the courage to compliment her. As soon as he began rising to the sky, he was already trying to formulate the words to say to her — although nothing much more than a "Hi," and a "You look beautiful," crossed his tongue. At least she would notice him — it was a rarity to run into her when he was this full. The thunderstorms kept blocking him every time he thought it would be the right time to finally say anything to her.

"Thank you," she said, naturally blushing.

"I'm sorry," the moon muttered. "I didn't mean to make things seem weird. You really do look beautiful."

There was a painfully awkward silence before she thanked him again.

Damn it, the moon thought to himself. *I don't have much time left.*

He looked up at her and his heart began accelerating. She looked down and around him, nervously, but it couldn't help the setting that he found her in. On usual afternoons, she would turn the clouds yellow until she began to inevitably dim, and finally, the moon would take her place in illuminating the sky.

But tonight was different.

The moon stared straight into her eyes, and although they wandered furiously, they met for split seconds at a time. Every time they did, the clouds and the trees and the skyscraper's windows sunk to an orange; then to a pink; and finally, to a deep red.

The moon decided that he had enough of these uncomfortable moments. It was her, in fact, who was the reason behind his own illumination; otherwise, nobody would even notice that he existed. Although he was nervous beyond belief, he couldn't resist catching her at this perfect moment in the sky. He looked at the world turn, and slowly but surely, he knew that without her none of them would even be able to live at all.

"I don't mean to be weird—"

She gasped as she turned the sky to a deep purple.

"Sorry, I—I don't mean to be weird or anything. But honestly, I'm still in love with you. I can still feel your radiation that filled in my craters; even the ones on the dark side. You did that. It feels amazing. I'm in love with you. I spin around the world in hopes to find you in the way that you were that night, but it's been years. We've been in the sky for only a short amount of time—but I want to spend the rest of my life with you. You alone can make me shine—even when you're not around for the world to see. But when we were in that moment, I know you felt something for me too. I don't know if this will make things different for us from not on—but I don't care. You mean everything to me. Otherwise, I would just an object made of dust. I'm sorry."

For a while, there was silence. The moon dipped himself into the golden hope that she gave him—but also submerged himself into the darkness of the universe. It was a frozen moment made of pure thought for the two of them.

The purple of the sky started to quickly fade back to her. She began slipping from his view.

"Say something," the moon begged. "I can't keep thinking like this without knowing how you feel."

There was a sad look on her face; a look full of authenticity, yet indulged in an internal struggle as if her insides battled each other in a powerful combustion.

As she sunk to just a sliver to the moon's brightening eye, she quietly — and to the moon, almost regretfully — whispered,

"I'm sorry, moon. I am the sun, and I always have, and always will, love the earth."

She disappeared into the horizon of the earth itself.

The moon hung silently, looking into the eyes of the earth itself. He gleamed in defeat.

It was the brightest night on record.

flowers to sunsets

i'll try to compare
flowers to sunsets

just how I long
for the memory
of your heart

six seconds

...aaaand stop.

In six seconds you will tell me goodbye. Everything you will do from the next moment on, until infinity, will have nothing to do with me ever again. One day 22.638 years from 'six seconds from now,' you will look back and bury your hands into your face wondering why you ever said goodbye to me 22.638 years from six seconds from now. Then, your tears will dry, and you will accept the fact that I was never meant to be anyway—and you will move on with your life.

Why did I choose to reflect six seconds from the moment you told me goodbye forever?

Because in that moment, that's when I'll know.

I will see it in your beautiful eyes that you will drop me off to the side of your world. Six seconds from the moment that you will say goodbye, tears will begin formulating in your eyelids and I will swear that my life will be dissolving in the reflection of your saline liquid.

God damn it. It will hit me like I am stretched across the train tracks when your roaring words will tear me apart. I will have no idea that it will come.

Sometimes I will think of you like I will seven seconds before it all happens. You'll have content silence. There will be a surprised smile on your face. You will be mine and you will be whole; but at the same time, you will complete. You will be permanent in a temporary lifetime

Sometimes I will see you eight seconds before it happens. You will laugh like I have tickled you—although it will be my words that causes your outburst instead of my fingers. Your eyes will light up like the first time they ever did. You will be close to me. You will be beautiful.

Sometimes I will see you nine seconds from now. You will be above me. You will have no idea this will come either. That's exactly what I will want—because, even if you will have no idea, you told me in the past, even on sober nights, that you would be ready to do this. God, you will be so beautiful to me.

On my knees, knowing that God will already say that you will nod your head up and down, I will ask you to be mine forever—ten seconds before you will tell me goodbye.

"Goodbye."

Goodbye.

a lesson

you may meet
a thousand people
who will make you believe
that love is inherited.

and they will all leave,
and then leave,
and then leave again,

until one
decides to stay
to teach you
that love
is to be learned,

before they, too,
will walk
out your door.

a boy with words

You love a boy with words.

One with a mouth and a stunning smile — one that captivates you from the instant you two meet. He's got a voice that wasn't afraid to approach you early on. One that laughs at your jokes and makes you laugh too; or maybe you're just nervous, so you laugh when you don't know what else to do with your voice.

Whether or not you know a thing about him, there's this energy that pulls you to him. It's enthralling. It pulsates. You're reeled in even before he shoots you that pickup line you've been expecting. And it's all great; your heart beats left and right instead of up and down for this boy who has a smile and a voice and some words that joke alongside your ears. And then things get real — real quick — and now he's into you.

But speed isn't a factor. Because he's different; he's special; he's something new; something else; he's into you. And that's different, because the people who used to be into you decided, without notification, that they weren't into you anymore.

So you say you're into him too. You say, "Yes, I'd love to go out with you. I'd love to be into you, while at the same time, I'm with you. You've got a mouth and a smile and words and jokes, and my god. I'm so captivated by that, and by the way — I'm into you."

And then one day, things get strange. Things about him feel fabricated. His smile is authentic as ever, except this time, he doesn't smile. His voice isn't excited when he talks to you.

Soon after, you notice that he's got a mouth with a smile with a voice with jokes for someone new. All of a sudden, you're not the new one — you're the old one. And you ask him if this is true.

So then, he uses your favorite feature about him — his words. Captivating, convincing, relentless, and always, always: the truth. And then he smiles. And jokes. And tells you that he is yours and also that he loves you and that you're wrong, even though you're right.

And you believe him without a doubt. Because maybe you don't actually love this boy. You just love the words that come out of his mouth in a world where there are fourteen billion ears.

a choke on ashes

Tell me,
when you
touched his lips,

did you feel the fire
that you once threw
into my lungs

that now leaves
my every sigh
for you
a choke on ashes?

count to three

There's a reason you'll read this and others won't. You're the type of person to be awake at this time, wandering aimlessly around the night with high hopes — but also with a low heart.

You'll sit around looking at the sky, begging for the answers. But tonight, the stars have nothing to say to you — so you'll have to carry on and deal with your own problems.

But you'll know that you can't. You'll know that from here on, things are going to get colder; the night will just only get darker; your heart will only hurt more. You'll try to not inhale deeply because it will hurt — but you'll do it every once in a while just to wonder if you are really feeling the things you think you are.

Then, all of a sudden, every breath will grow longer, slower, and more painfully. You'll be stuck at the edge of your earth; at the corner of a waterfall; with no current. You'll look down, and it'll be a lot farther than it will be from up.

But something will pull you away from the top; something connected to the bottom of your heart. You'll be a cigarette halfway burnt into a butt. You'll suffocate as if your tears couldn't escape out of your face. And you'll sit down, with trembling fingers, and you'll end up reading this.

And it won't help, but it won't hurt. It won't be good or bad — it'll just there. And so then, you'll just sit in the gray, as still as a rock — at a pause.

You'll count to three and hold your breath.

One,
Two,
Three,

;

A boy pulls up in the parking lot. He sees a girl walking away from her car. He gets out of the car as fast as he can—he has not embraced her for weeks.

She slows her path—they have not intersected paths for weeks.

"I'm so happy to see you," the boy says, smiling, with an ounce of unrefined desperation.

"It's good to see you too," the girl says, as she equally distributes her smile in accordance to him.

He looks at her for a moment as if he took medicine to calm himself down.

She stares at his feet with a clenched jaw as if she were staring at a hole in the ear—although, maybe, she was looking at the sky since she felt like she was at the bottom of the world already.

He cannot help but hug her because he cannot not waste an opportunity to carry the weight of his heart for this last time.

She cannot help but hug him back.

His endorphins sprint to his heart as his face buries into her hair.

She feels an emptiness in the embrace; in whispers, she counts the seconds behind his back that will later be added onto the list of *moving on*.

Over the boy's soggy soul, the mask plastered onto his face to maintain his composure finally breaks.

"I love you," he says, which sounds like he is hesitant; but inside, he doesn't hesitate to say it one bit.

"I . . .,"

The mask over the girl's throat breaks loose.

"I love you for you—that's what you first told me," he says, panting. Maybe he says this as a line of defense for the silence that grazes part his heart—although it still beats in her direction.

"You only love parts of me," she finally blurts out without much conviction—although her heart does not hesitate like her tongue does.

He lets go of the hug and watches the pupils in her eyes turn into a hole in the earth—although maybe it was the sky, because he felt like he was at the bottom of the world already.

She sees his soul fold.

"I tried," he says, a withered tremble.

"You couldn't do it," she says, solidified.

"Could you love all of yourself?" he asks—a final stand before his heart erupts in defeat once more.

She does not say yes.

The conversation ends. It does not make them happy, give them closure, or rest them in peace. It is just there, like how flies buzz in between eyes. It ends with a pause, not a stop;

nothing but what we could have been

A year ago I used to look at the stars on cloudless winter nights. Nobody really told me to look at the stars — but nobody really did anyway. Nobody had to. They just had to observe the world, and eventually, on the right night, they would see nothing but black — except for the universe that hid above them for fourteen out of the twenty four hours that they would cycle through — and then they would look up.

That's how I ended up staring at the sky for five out of those fourteen hidden hours every night. I didn't remember the first time I saw it, but I figured out that, if you looked long enough, you'd eventually catch the flare of a shooting star.

After I found the first split second phenomenon, they were the only thing I looked for.

Eventually summer had come — with ghosts of humidity and exhales of heat. The skies closed into shields of condensation every night, so I stopped looking up.

But I kept looking for shooting stars. I had no idea what I was looking for other than a streak in a clouded sky. By the end of summer I had looked as long and as far as forever could be in a finite amount of time. Yet I found nothing but the shade of night — even in the broad of day.

But that was the day I met you.

And when I met you, there was no more phenomenon of the stars that streaked finitely across the canvas of clear skies. There was no longing to search for the complexity of the universe.

I met a shooting star in the flesh of a human being.

When I spoke to you, my heart raced faster than the showers I had once waited for. There were rays of light in our conversations instead of streaks of luminescence that lasted for merely half of a blink.

I was in love.

But just like shooting stars, you too seemed to fade into nothingness—I was left searching for something as intangible as the soul that had streaked its way into my heart. Maybe I was blinded by the tiny illumination of your presence in a sky that was too black for far too long; but nevertheless, the sensation of your wholeness infected my heart.

And as I looked into the sky tonight for the first time since forever ago, I saw the same stars—and felt nothing but what we could've been.

perceiving me wrong

love is
the most universal language
on this earth
yet somehow
you got lost
in my translation

july

I'm sitting 37 minutes into third period, smack in the middle of September of my junior year of high school. I'm sitting in this class on a Tuesday—the slowest fucking day to exist in the public school system—and usually, I would've been grinding my ass off to the music of the second hand on the wall; but today, my mind has been panting nostalgia from a day in July.

As I look around, while everyone else in the class sleeps, I meet a girl's eyes who is presumably delving in the same activities as I am. Her eyes have this electrifying glare that I've recognized in someone else's.

As she looks at me, my heart begins under metamorphic-like temperatures, and suddenly, the clock isn't the only thing that's ticking in the room.

The walls of the room begin melting into darkness—sporadically, a summer humidity blankets over my lungs. My voice starts to disappear along with the rest of the dormant souls that once infested the classroom that I was just sitting in—everyone except for this girl—and I don't even know her because I never cared to. But now I'm thinking that I should've—now that this whole paranormal event is taking place.

We end up sitting in a field. It shouldn't be after nine o' clock, because the heat hasn't broken yet. And it's just me and this stranger, still in our desks, and there are stars in the sky that shine brighter than my dreams. I look back down at her and she's still looking at me with this glare. She hasn't said a word, as her face regresses into a relaxed state.

She begins to slide out from her desk towards me. At this point, I don't know what the hell to do; as far as I know, I'm sitting thirty seven minutes into third period.

She arrives at my desk, bends down, puts her fingers onto my arm, one by one, and kisses my lips, groove on groove, and just before she can look me in the eyes, she whispers something unrecognizable into my ears.

Confused, I open my eyes. This girl's face, nose, lips—all an inch away from mine. But I know these eyes, and they're not hers.

Because suddenly, it all makes sense.

"We may not last the summer, but you will regret the day you realize that you gave up on me."

It is 38 minutes into third period, and I am left in last summer's comma.

friends

one day
you will thank change
for being the better friend

because forever
may give you
a hopeful promise
but it always
be one
that ends

the one who got away is still the one

Somewhere, out there, I was still searching for you. I swam through the seas because the waves whispered your name. I opened my mouth and whispered your name back although you would never respond after that. But I kept whispering until there was enough water in my lungs to drown.

I figured that after months of aimlessly searching — and hoping — for the rarity of the moment when I would find a dot of ink in an infinitely blank page that you were not here in the ocean. Perhaps you stopped sinking and decided to fly.

I reached the horizon of the water and the sky — where I am now. I stopped my search for you; for if you had decided to jump straight from the sea into the sky, then the possibility of finding you now would be nearly impossible as compared to finding you in a limited container of water.

But I remembered that if you had given me lungs, you damn well had given me wings.

The sky is only infinite to ones who do not fly.

My search for you goes on.

how to move on when you are the only one

if you think
you are valiant
then you are blinded
in stupidity

if you think you are
stupid
then what a valiant thing
it is
to accept it

thanks

This year, I'll be giving thanks to the past more than the present.

After ringing the doorbell outside of the neighbor's home, I'll walk up to warmer days, when the light was a lot friendlier than how it is now — but when the night was tremendously darker and hours longer.

I'll even give it a hug — although at that time, when the sun's rays barely touched my skin through window cracks, I'll feel a forest fire spread through the hairs on my arm into the fibers of my heart.

When it's time to raise the first glass, I'll thank all the times I threw the rock down the newly-formed well in the second half of heart, expecting to hear a splash — but every single time; dried earth colliding with one another was always the auditory result. I'll remember how I would scream back at my hollowed soul in response for anyone to hear me. I'm sure many people did, but it didn't mean anything if it wasn't her.

As the turkey is being cut, I'll thank all the times I would look back on every love letter that once graced my heart during the first read-around. But after, every letter I read had sliced every perception of the "love-of-my-life-forever-and-ever-amen" that had grown in my hands for years. After that moment, I wrapped my lips over several others, yet my soul did not follow my actions. Instead, it hovered over me instead of filling in the emotional grooves that had steadily widened for months.

Once dinner is over, and the party is left dormant on the living room couches, I'll thank the tranquility that I was left with; one would think that a quiet room would be peaceful — no distractions, no noise, no fast movements. But I need chaos. I need flashing lights, I need wailing cacophonies from every radial direction, I need life to speed past me — otherwise, my thoughts would choke on every flat-lined tranquility out of my soul with slow, screaming reminders of loneliness for eternities; however, in reality, all of this would be contained in a thought that would last for a couple seconds. And that is what happened every hour of every day for months.

When the night is done, I'll thank her. A girl who is just a someone now; a memory; a past that isn't a present this year, but one who was one last year. I thanked her then, and I'll thank her now.

Except I won't actually thank her. I won't ring her doorbell. I won't drink her wine. I won't kiss her lips or write her love letters or call her my forever. I won't sit on her couch with her on my chest without saying a word; without anything saying anything at all.

This year, I'll give thanks to everything I gave thanks for last year—except, instead of the past giving thanks for this future, the future that is the present now will be giving thanks to the past.

Will I feel complete this year?

Will I actually be giving thanks, or will I actually just stick my head in clouds that, emotionally, consist of nostalgia?

Yes.
No.
Yes.
No.

let's run away

"Let's run away."

That's what she told him the night before she left in the summer. They were both fourteen when she urged him to leave the stagnant, safe world that they both existed in.

She came from a family that was in a constant tumble of wreckage throughout the past five years. Her mother and father were divorced. The year after the split, there was a constant rotation of various men that packed in and out of her tiny ocean-side home. Four out of five men had come with arms tied around her mother with preconceived notions of finding a partner for life. Within eight or nine months, they left without any doubt that they had made a mistake. One even left with a gaping hole in the decade-old drywall of the main bedroom. It was, of course, filled by the next prospect of her mother's romantic life—the current one—controlling and dominant, just like the last four.

"But what about our families?"

He came from a family that was privileged beyond measure. His mother and father were as happy as ever— at least that's what the public saw. The two parents bonded with their single son only after they tended their weekend vacations across the bay, always leaving him at their vacation house by the sea. When they came back, the only conversation they held with him was just as superficial as the conversations that they grasped onto in order to keep their positive reputation to the tiny coastal community alive.

Although he was bothered greatly by this, his parents gave him everything he asked for. They were his only form of exposure to the word. Until he met her, all that he knew were puppy dog eyes, puppy dog eyes, puppy do—

"Don't you want your life to be any different?"

She glared at him as she clenched at the border of his windowsill.

"Why do you look at me like that?"

He'd seen those eyes gleam before. He'd fallen in love with them in the last four months, but he hadn't told her.

"Because—I know you. You don't want to stay here. You're forgotten, just like me."

She was getting desperate.

There was a silence between them. She looked down.

"What can I do to convince you to go with me?" she asked, eyes still pointed at his fingers.

He said nothing.

He looked into her eyelids. Not too long ago, she had begun to brush a shade as dark and as mysterious as their clear, oceanic skies.

He blinked,

He blinked,

He bl—

There they were—eyes, rich caramel. Sometimes, in the sun they surpassed the shade of golden.

She grabbed his shirt intensely.

Stunned, his own eyes spread wide.

Both of them with eyes closed again, she pulled him in—fast at first, like after the climax of a roller coaster. But as they became within inches of each other, their rate of intersection came into fractions, then infinite decimals.

As his eyes opened to see what had happened between them, her eyes did too.

Caramel, he thought. But right now, all he noticed were her pupils. The aperture of hers was wider than any that he'd ever seen before.

"Puppy dog eyes."

Puppy dog eyes.

"What?" she asked in a whispered notation, confused almost to the point of offense.

"You're giving me puppy dog eyes."

"What do you mean?"

A silence interrupted, swallowing the emotions that had filled both of their hearts.

There was a frown on her lips, only two inches from his.

"I'm sorry. I can't go with—"

And just like that, she had dropped from his window and disappeared from his life. He stuck his head out the window and screamed her name pleading her to not go, but nobody was there to listen. She was gone into the night.

Four summers later, just as he was packing his belongings for his first semester in college in his vacation home of his now separated parents, he noticed a knocking sound at his window. It was familiar; one he'd been waiting around for the past couple of years.

Her.

She managed to pull herself up to the windowsill, then into his room.

Her eyes were gleaming, just the same as before. They were never puppy dog eyes from the start. He was at a loss for words.

"I—I'm sorry. I should have never stayed here. I should have left with you."

She blinked with the same night skies that had first brushed her skin.

She blinked with the same eyes that spoke the only truth she ever knew.

Without much thought, the lips of every word that came out of their soul, every truth, every lie, every word that was or wasn't meant, had met.

"I should have never left you."

come closer

"Come closer," she said with her lips and hook of a finger that creased in and out.

She was across the room. I knew her well, but I wasn't shit compared to all the other guys she would always date for months at a time.

Every time I'd see her over the years I'd smile and tell her hello. Sometimes I'd get lucky if we happened to be walking to lunch at the same time.

I'd strategically place my steps to be in front of hers just to open the door for her. I craved her smile. I craved to hear the melody of her voice sing into my ears with simple lyrics as "Thank you." or "aw." But there was never a time where I could introduce my name to her, even though I knew her name for years on end.

"Come closer," she said with a smile on her face and a grace in her voice. She was a couple bodies away from me in a crowded room. I knew she was talking to me. She had singled out my own two eyes — I was sure of it. I swear she spelled out my name.

There was music blaring my ears out and sweat that could be collected with buckets pouring out of me. I wasn't a party type of person; I was just looking out for one of my friends.

He turned out to be okay I think. I didn't really remember anything past her telling me,

"Come closer."

She was right in front me now. I trembled at the presence of her comfort. My heart had swelled to my throat. I barely exerted a "hello" back to her.

She laughed.

I wasn't sure if it was at me or with me, but I didn't laugh back.

"What?" she said with a smile on her face. She was beautiful, but I wasn't sure why she'd think to approach me.

"Do you even know my name?"

She laughed again.

"Of course I know your name. I know that you look at me in class. I know that you walk faster than me to lunch to open the doors. I know that you're nervous when you tell me hello. I know that you care."

She looked at my lips and grabbed my hand.

"Come closer."

I put down her drink. Alcohol.

There's a toxic part about the heart sometimes with similar effects as alcohol.

"You won't remember this by the morning," I told her. Only I would.

"Come closer."

celebrate

Sixteen years old sitting in the corner of a wedding party, everybody is drunk beyond fucking words, dancing their hearts away for the bride and groom, plastered with obligatory but genuine smiles, and everything is perfect in their world, but tonight my heart does not flow with the waves of happy people. Tonight my heart isn't even in the same ocean. Don't get me wrong though; the people are beautiful. The newly-wed couple is beautiful. The world is beautiful.

But I'm sixteen years old, sitting in the corner of a wedding party, and I'm sober enough for cycles of chaptered thoughts, sitting as still as the romantic pulse in my heart, thinking about irrelevant souls that once entered the laces of my heart. Tonight my heart sinks to the bottom of a trench that I forgot I had.

Because it's been too long since I've thought about the girls who said they loved me. It's been too long since I've thought about the same ones that I've painstakingly rejected.

Today I saw two souls look into each other's eyes, creating a connection to a bond that was stronger than any emotional bridge that I had crossed — with eyes that spoke more words in half a second than any that I had written in an entire lifetime. And it made every heart swell — every heart including mine. But mine was different.

Because I'm sixteen years old,
Lying in the corner of my heart,
drunk on love with nobody to share it with,
and I miss being in love like a stone wishes to float in an ocean filled with waves.

i still think about you

When the sun began setting at five in the afternoon for the first time, it seemed as if I hadn't noticed it when it happened last year. When I was with you.

I still think about you — the version of you that I last remember. I think about the warmth of your skin when everything was frozen. I think of your breath when you whispered confidence into my soul. I think about your scent that wrapped around my heart and churned it into butter. I think of accepting the completion of my existence when I repeated three words in your direction. Every insecurity I had was observed, acknowledged, and left unjudged by you.

You were good to me.

But when a good exists one day and then disappears the next, we search for replacements — or improvements. Sometimes we find them — in ourselves, or in others — and sometimes we're left with shortened wrists and trembling, emptied fingers.

I still think about this concept sometimes; us, as a fate that had a beginning, middle, and end. But it turns out that wasn't the truth. We won't have an end together, and if we did, it was at a time where I went on and you didn't. But that doesn't stop me from thinking about a you that exists in another universe where you're laying across from me in a bed in six o'clock darkness of the winter. A you that stapled comfort into my bones instead of one that ran out of things to say. A you that I could whisper secrets into instead of screaming small talk with. A you that makes me grateful that we met. A you that I started something with.

A you from the past.

I still think about you, and it doesn't hurt. But I still think about you, and even if it were the end of me who ended up alone, I still would, knowing that a version of you who was mine is still out there — if not here anymore.

not poetry

i am happy
and i don't know you
but if there are thoughts
that find comfort
in your sadness
i swear
that those thoughts are evil
and they shouldn't be me
even if they were you
when things were different

campout

I saw the stars tonight.

It was away from the city — into the mountains. It had been a long time since I was there. I was a twelve year old boy in seventh grade looking for a group to fit in when I last stepped foot on this campground. I was quiet, shy, and timid before I spoke to my peers. When I did, it was only because I had to or when someone was awaiting a response after they asked me a question. While other immature middle schoolers shot jokes out each other's mothers or told each other rumors about penises, I was the one who was the first to sit around the fire until the entire group surrounded the flames in the night's tranquility.

We sat there and watched the light of energy dissipate onto our bodies to keep warm. We'd look up and see the skies, and all the stars from home would be there. But there would be hundreds of thousands more to fill in the spaces from the regularly scheduled pulsars. We would ask which constellations were which: belts, warriors, scorpions, dippers, and the older ones would tell us, but we'd never really understand. The sky was so vast and so pure that we were too young to understand, so we'd just look back down into the simplicity of the fire, flame after flame.

Tonight, back in the same campground, I am a 16 year old boy in his junior year of high school, the majority of my conversations with adults include what my future is going to look like — to which I reply an interest that seems like a logical field of work, but really, I have no idea what I want to do for the rest of my life. I have homework that could drown me in both physical and emotional quantities, I have tests that determine my intellectual legitimacy, and I have unnecessary stress because I often fear failure in everything.

Tonight, I sat by the flames—the same ones that I sat by four and a half years ago as one of only two or three "old kids." The middle schoolers continued to say "your mom" jokes and talked about dangling body parts.

I was still quiet. I looked down at the fire just as everyone eventually did as the night progressed. I looked up at the stars. I hadn't seen them like this in so long. My soul had grown so fully since then; my life had shifted in unimaginable ways. I would have never seen the way I turned out to be four and a half years ago.

"Which one is Orion?" a kid asked. But I didn't know. I looked up, I saw the stars, and I had no idea what I was looking at. I didn't know a thing about the sky after all this time. Even then, I was beautiful. I didn't look at the fire for the rest of the night.

nobody

Four years ago, you saw her. You were young when you first laid eyes on her. It was from afar, among a crowd of people—an audience—and she was stage left in the grand scheme of things. You, seated on the right side of the auditorium, thought she was the center attraction; so did all the other kids who were sitting with you. And although you were young, you knew that you wanted her to be in your life. You were in love with her from the get-go. Although shy, although hesitant, although quiet, you were enthralled. She didn't notice you at all; that didn't matter. Her existence alone established itself in your thoughts, and that was enough to notice her in every chapter of your life.

A year later, you find yourself in the same room as her. She's got her back towards you for motifs that seem almost intentional against you. You're disappointed by this—she's not who you imagined her to be. You stand up, push your seat in, turn around to exit the room, and right before you take your first step away from her entire existence in your life, you hear,

"Hey."

It's her. You say hello back and the conversation begins. She's actually noticed you before even though she never said a thing about it. You're into her more now than ever.

A year passes. She's everything who you thought she was, and then some more. You ask to be in a relationship with her. You're committed; she is too. It has been a year of new experiences for you to realize that she's worth more than one cycle over. You realize something:

"I love you."

"I love you too."

She loves you too.

Two more years pass, and you still continue to love her. She does too.

But things are going to be different after this.

They're going to change. You and she are going to end. And there's nothing you can do but live out the final moments. You only start crying until the second to last memory you will ever have of her. When the last moment passes, that's it. It's done; she and you will never be each other's again for the rest of your lives. You could have stayed completely still for the entire duration of the four years being with her, but the geography of the emotional world would still grow a mountain in between the two of you.

An hour after the end, you sit alone in a crowd full of people. You sit on the right side of the auditorium. She stands stage left. You love her, but only from afar. Things had to end. And nothing new has or will start — *at least not for a while,* you tell yourself.

So for now, you're nobody. You're not hers anymore. You're not your own; you've given so much of you to her for so long that you can't be what you used to be prior to being hers. You belong to no one, floating endlessly into whatever next builds its roots into your soul.

psychopath

some days
i do not write
i just tremble
with a pen in my hand
and by the end
it is not art
it is just a list
of things to say
as my madness radiates
knowing
that someone
will find it beautiful

quiet

I've been quiet.

I wake up and roll out of bed. I stumble to the shower, turn on the water and wait for a minute and thirty seconds for the water to warm up. I shower for forty minutes (always) while staring at the tile in front of me. There's grout in between, but not enough for me to add 'clean grout from the shower tiles' to my list of things to do on the weekend.

Forty minutes later, I continue stumbling, but this time, to the sink. The mirror stares at me staring at the mirror. I floss and brush. I walk back to my room, change into my clothes, put my bags on, get into my car, and drive to school.

I get there; I'm five minutes late. I walk in while the pledge falls from the groggy mouths of the kids in my school. I knock on my classroom door. My teacher opens it; everyone stares. I stare back.

The day goes on.

My friends make jokes about everything. I chuckle, I scoff, but not enough to laugh. The things they say are funny, but so is everything if someone really thinks about funny things hard enough. I'm not generally comedic anyway.

I walk through the hallways between classes. I see the assholes, I see the kids that the assholes wrap around, I see the kids watching all of this and not caring. I see the couples sucking face like love in youth is going to last forever. I understand why they do it. I understand why all of them do these things. I understand that they'll be me one day, understanding why they used to be these things.

I drive home, I nap, I eat dinner, I do my homework, I go to bed.

These are my usual days. I've been quiet; I say words, but I haven't actually said anything in a good while. I've got thoughts, such as "I wish I weren't here anymore," or "I wish I were in love again." But I can't change those things for now.

So I just sit. I observe. I take it all in. Although life is slow for now, it doesn't mean that life is terrible. There is beauty in fade.

There is solace in whispers.

So I've been quiet.

But I've been happy, knowing that things are about to go into hyper-speed; with life, with love, with family, with growth, with me.

All at once; all by myself, all with life.

glasses

There are certain people that you will meet along the timeline of your life that will make you see the world as if you are wearing a pair of glasses.

The first time you receive a pair of these glasses could be early on in your youth, or well on into your teenage years.

Regardless of the age, there is a striking innocence correlated with your first pair. You will see things you have never felt before. The second you realize that you are captivated by a soul that you think you have known since the start of your existence just by looking into their suddenly translucent eyes, you will begin to realize that you have been living a life full of romance and emotion blindly up until this very moment. You will most likely not be able to recall this moment in your life, but from then on you will know that there is an existence of the thing that romantically bonds billions of people existing on this earth.

But this clearness will come way too fast and way too swift to last for a sustainable amount of time, and before you know it you will forget about the one who made you see so clearly.

The next time you receive a pair of these glasses is the second most important pair you will ever receive in your life. This pair will be given to you randomly, and soon you won't even have time to wonder how you saw the world the original glasses you possessed. This pair of glasses will make you see vibrancy in the oranges of the fall, the whites of the winter, and the greens on the spring. They will make you see defined lines instead of blurs, corners instead of curves, and skylines instead of bleeding horizons.

This pair of glasses will make you look into the mirror and see a stranger that you will grow accustomed to, because after a while, you will realize that you are looking at the person that this pair of glasses helped form into. And just when you think you have reached the perfect vision, you will start to see dots forming in the grays of the walls. You will see grains of sand on the sides of mountaintops. You will begin to notice the fade of unbearable colors, and you will grow hungry to feel the emotions that this pair of glasses once made you feel.

But no matter how many times that you will blink, or how hard you close your eyes, your vision will grow worse — worse enough to decide that it is time to move on. And even though this pair of glasses has made you see the world in a way you didn't see before, you know what is best for you, and you decide to look for a better pair.

From here, it does not get easier. At first you will grow desperate, and you will try every pair that you can get your hands on at first glance — pairs that you know will never be suitable for seeing the world that you want to see. But out of heartache and disappointment, you decide to do it anyway. And with every pair, you begin to see the world in a different way, every time.

Because when you look into a pair of glasses, you see the world in their point of view, whether you listen or not.

Sometimes you will end up throwing the wrong pairs down at a first glance, but other times you end up being entranced because of the desire to see difference in your life. You will see things you are pressured to look at and you will find demons waiting at the shores of the clouds. You will see shadows in the between the rays of the sun. You will find a home in the darkness. And you will claim that this is the world that you want to see, but in reality, this is the world that you have accepted.

Because you have lost the way.

And once you realize this, you will decide to throw these glasses onto the ground. But the colors and shapes still remain in your vision.

And you will look to the sky, and you will still see the ground. You will look at the ocean, and you will see the desert. You will look at hope, and you will see nothing at all.

And in the darkest of the nights, in the darkest of the days, you will find the shards of broken glass and strips of torn wire in the corners of a cave that you have been lying in since you fell.

Maybe it will take weeks, or maybe even months, but you will soon realize that you have the ability to create your own pair. And before long, with your own hands, you will have created your own vision of perfection.

That is when you will learn to find yourself.

To fall in love, alone.

sore fingers

today in its dust
i played my guitar for the first time in years;
i did not forget the chords
or how to strum
or how to sing
but my fingers grew weary
and began enduring the pain
of the strings that pushed
into the tenderness
of my skin
but it was music nonetheless

i cannot apologize for
the pain that i feel
i cannot contain the emotions
that crawl from my fingers
as if i have been possessed;
i must be an unfiltered demon
in order to survive

i cannot apologize
for crawling back to art

i will always be searching for you

The seconds tick louder than words that I've internally screamed at the physical volume contained inside my watch.

You and I—we haven't known each other for long. And very soon, we will no longer know one another. That's the beauty of time; in one way it's separating us, and in another, it bonds us.

You know this fact just as well as I do. But you've remained prevalent in my heart, just as I have inside yours.

And now time has lead up to this moment, a moment defined as "the end" of our existence being hand in hand—together emotionally—flying freely side by side.

I look up to discover your facial expressions unlike the ones that I normally find during the end of a relationship. You have a smile on your face that looks bittersweet; a smile that maybe was a frown when I wasn't looking, but a smile that has grown exuberant the instant my eyes meet yours.

And in this moment, I see your eyes, I see the blush on your skin, and I see your smile contract into an emotion that makes me see you as more than just a person that I know—and soon a person that I only once knew.

In this moment, the seconds grow increasingly louder.

In this moment, the seconds grow progressively longer as a reminder that not everything lasts forever; instead, life is full of moments.

Moments like these;

A single second that can change the emotional structure of one's heart for the rest of their life.

And when your lips meet mine, your soul departs from me at the same exact second.

Because this is the end of us. The end of you and me, me and you, mine and yours.

This is the end.

And although I will still taste the sound of our moment for hours upon months after today, I will crave the single second that has made us infinite.

I will long for the stopping of time.

I will always be searching for you.

thank you for everything

from frank

The next page that you will read is the beginning of a story; my story. Yours, too. It will soon be ours. Although this story may seem grand — although it may leave an imprint on you as permanent as ink on this page — it is a story that will not last forever. It will end. We are small. 'Forever' may mean forever to you and me, but to others it is nothing but a moment suspended in time before reality begins moving again. This is what this story is. This is what we were, are, and will be. This book is a forever that will last for infinity and not at all — at the same exact time. This is the story of how we fell in love; how we fell out of it; and how we forgot about its entire existence. This is the story of the next us, the one after that — and so on. If 'us' was formerly you and I, we are still 'us' if it is just me; if it is just you. This story was a forever to two people — at least for a moment in eternity. Although this is a forever that ends, it will live forever. This is how. It is just a speck of ink among a sentence among a paragraph among a chapter among an entire novel. This is what we are. It may be uncomfortable to some, but it is definitely necessary to the completion of our entire lifetimes. So — this is us. A forever suspended in time; a pause; a silence,

    — to the reader, writer, and doer,
       — from the past, present, and future

afterthoughts

This book is meant to be read at different moments in your lifetime. Like the yearbooks that will gather dust in your childhood bedroom, the personal meaning of this book to you has the ability to change a personal meaning from one point in your lifetime to another. You may find yourself reading this book at the beginning of budding relationship; other times, you may find yourself reading this book at the bottom of heartbreak. This book was made to transform under your perspective of life.

Make this story your own. These poems and short stories are someone else's, but the story is yours. It doesn't have to be the book in its entirety; you will naturally pick and choose which pieces speak the most to you.

And remember—your personal story to this book may be subject to change. You may read this story again in ten years, and the mosaic that you will paint in your head will be completely different than the one you have just created.

about the author

Nash Consing is a poet, artist, and creator on the brink of transition into adulthood. He currently distributes pats to his three dogs, Jerome, Xavier, and Yoda, at least fifty times a day.

Follow @nashconsing on Instagram for more poetry, updates, and quotes.

about the cover artist

Ruth Cabahug is a young artist from New Zealand. She aspires to inspire people through her artwork.

Follow @expressiquee on Instagram for her illustrations.

Made in the USA
Middletown, DE
16 June 2017